JITENDRA – LOST CONNECTIONS

IN SEARCH OF A THERAPIST

Series Editors: Michael Jacobs and Moira Walker

JITENDRA – LOST CONNECTIONS

Edited by Michael Jacobs

OPEN UNIVERSITY PRESS
Buckingham • Philadelphia

Open University Press
Celtic Court
22 Ballmoor
Buckingham
MK18 1XW

and
1900 Frost Road, Suite 101
Bristol, PA 19007, USA

First Published 1996

A catalogue record of this book is available from the British Library

ISBN 0 335 19242 4 (pb)

Library of Congress Cataloging-in-Publication Data
Jitandra—lost connections / edited by Michael Jacobs.
     p.   cm.—(In search of a therapist)
   ISBN 0–335–19242– 4 (pbk.)
   1. Psychotherapy — Case studies. 2. Jitendra. I. Jacobs,
Michael, 1941– . II. Series.
RC465.J58 1996
616.89'14—dc20   95–51047
                                             CIP

Typeset by Graphicraft Typesetters Limited, Hong Kong
Printed in Great Britain by St Edmundsbury Press,
Bury St Edmunds, Suffolk

CONTENTS

THE EDITOR AND CONTRIBUTORS

Bernard Burgoyne is a psychoanalyst practising in London. He is a founder member of the Centre for Freudian Analysis and Research, and a member of the European School of Psychoanalysis. He is the course leader of the MA in psychoanalysis, and the Head of the Centre for Psychoanalysis at Middlesex University. His research interests concern the relations between Lacan's formulations of psychoanalysis and those of Freud.

Fay Fransella is Director of the Centre for Personal Construct Psychology and Emeritus Reader in clinical psychology at the University of London. She trained as a clinical psychologist and has worked as a full-time research psychologist and university teacher in London medical schools. She is known internationally for her work with personal construct psychology, and has written several books on the subject.

Josna Pankhania is a founder member of the Association of Black Counsellors. She works with a black feminist perspective and is interested in politicized counselling. She is Indian, born in East Africa and currently works part-time as a lecturer in community and youth studies at the University of the West of England. She is the author of *Liberating the National History Curriculum* (Falmer Press).

Christopher Perry is a training analyst of the Society of Analytical Psychology, a training therapist and supervisor of the British Association of Psychotherapists, and a full member of the Group Analytic Society (London). He is author of *Listen to the Voice Within: A Jungian Approach to Pastoral Care* (SPCK) and of several articles on analytical psychology and group analysis. He is in private practice and teaches on a number of psychotherapy training courses.

Neil Rothwell is a clinical psychologist who has been working in the NHS in Scotland since qualifying thirteen years ago. Until recently, he worked with adults experiencing mental health problems and now works in a unit for head-injured adults with challenging behaviour. He is also a practising Buddhist and teacher of Buddhist meditation.

Diana Whitmore is Chairperson of the Psychosynthesis and Education Trust, a member of its Professional Training Board and a senior trainer and supervisor in psychosynthesis. She is a BAC-accredited supervisor and on the UKCP National Register. She co-founded the Association for Accredited Psychospiritual Psychotherapists. She has trained professionals throughout Europe and is a lecturer in psychosynthesis and psychospiritual subjects. She is author of *A Guide to the Joy of Learning: Psychosynthesis in Education* (Thorsons) and *Psychosynthesis Counselling in Action* (Sage).

Michael Jacobs is Director of the Psychotherapy and Counselling Programme at the University of Leicester, a psychotherapist registered with the UK Council for Psychotherapy and a Fellow of the British Association for Counselling. Apart from his clinical practice, he also writes on counselling and psychotherapy, being especially known for *The Presenting Past* (Open University Press) and *Psychodynamic Counselling in Action* (Sage).

And Jitendra, whose contribution forms the core of this book, has for obvious reasons to remain anonymous, although much of his life story is told in full in these pages.

MICHAEL JACOBS AND MOIRA WALKER

SERIES EDITORS' PREFACE

Take five clients, and for each client take six therapists. How will the therapists, or in one case the supervisors as well, understand and work with the following situations?

Charlie is a 40-year-old secretary to a Trades Union official, married with three children:

> I think of myself as someone who lacks self-confidence and feels she always has to apologize for herself, and I'm very insecure. The mildest row with my husband and I think he's going to leave me, and he finds that very irritating, I think. Understandably. I would. Having thought about it, I blame my mother for that. I use the word 'blame' quite consciously, because all the while I very much got the impression when I was young that she didn't love me and doesn't love me. I think of myself as unlovable.

Jitendra is a male Indian psychiatrist, separated from his Irish wife:

> One thing that . . . interests me and sometimes worries me is my early years, my childhood years. I have very few memories of anything before the age of six or five, but I am sure that they have left some legacy behind, a significant legacy, and sometimes I have deep feelings of sadness or complexity or ambivalence which are not immediately ascribable to events happening around me. And I wonder what these . . . what this augurs? I think a therapist might . . . help me in this area. The other area that I am wanting to understand is the dynamics of a large extended family . . . I would like to understand a little bit more about what affects a person's growing up in that context.

Morag is an accountant, the director of a catering business, a mother, stepmother and partner:

I feel that James wants me to be in the house, to be there because his children are there, and the family's there. He's quite happy to go off and play rugby on Sunday but he likes me being there being the mother-hen . . . I get quite cross, that he keeps trying to push me into the traditional role. I don't feel I've got on as far as I could have done had I been a man, because I had to work twice as hard as everybody else to get where I got . . . I feel OK always wanting to do something, but it does seem to cause quite a lot of conflict in my life. I feel, 'Is it right that I should always be wanting something new to go at, some new challenge? Should I just be accepting the way I am?'

Peta is an unemployed art teacher living in London:

I've got a problem with men. At least that's the way that I conceptualize it for the moment. I don't know whether it's a problem with other things as well, but over the last few weeks, particularly – which is a different thing from deep background, I suppose you'd say – some issues seem to have come into my mind that are to do with the fact that I am a woman and they men . . . It's rather difficult to know where to start, except that I feel very self-conscious and rather uncomfortable about the fact that I must also tell you that I'm a feminist. And also that my father was emotionally very distant.

Ruth was abused as a young girl. She wants to hold her male therapist. What can he say when she says to him?

Your reaction was – or I perceived it as being – a stand-off, and be cold to it, and not let anything happen, which obviously I understand; but I think it just highlighted that my desire . . . is not going to be matched by anyone else's. How can I communicate where I'm at, and help somebody else to understand that, and not necessarily to capitulate to me but just to be understanding?

This unique series of books takes a client's story, his or her presenting difficulties, the current situation, and some of the history from an initial session, recorded verbatim and printed in full for the reader to use. In the first four books, the session has been presented to six different therapists. They address their questions to the client, and explain in each book how they understand the client, how they want to work with the client, what further information they requested, and in the light of what they know, how they forecast the course of therapy. The reader is presented with six possible interpretations and working methods to compare and contrast, with a final telling response from the client and the editor on each of the therapists.

This series takes a further step forward from the comparative approaches of Rogers and others on film, or the shorter case vignettes in the *British Journal of Psychotherapy*, which have both been deservedly so popular with students and practitioners alike. All the therapists start with precisely the same information, which comes from a largely non-directed initial hour with four real clients. The reader can see in detail how each therapist takes it from there. How they share similar and contrasting insights and interpretations of the same person proves a remarkable and fascinating study of how different therapists work.

The final volume in the series goes a step further and submits one session of the editor's work with a long-term client to five different supervisors. How do they interpret the verbatim material? What questions do they want to ask the therapist? How do they advise the therapist to proceed? In this detailed insight into the work of a therapist and supervisors from different orientations, the reader gets an in-depth view of the value of supervision.

The five volumes in the series are entitled *Charlie – An Unwanted Child?*, *Peta – A Feminist's Problems with Men*, *Morag – Myself or Mother-hen?*, *Jitendra – Lost Connections* and, finally, *In Search of Supervision*.

1

IN SEARCH OF THE CLIENT

Just how different is the approach used by a therapist from one particular training society from that of a therapist from another orientation? In recent years, there has been much more interest in comparing approaches than in competing approaches. It is sometimes suggested that different methods may suit different clients, or even that therapists tend to select out the clients they can best work with.

There have been other attempts to demonstrate the way in which therapists from different schools might work with the same client. For many years, the two series of short films *Three Approaches to Psychotherapy*, the first made with Rogers, Perls and Ellis and the client 'Gloria', and the second with Rogers, Shostrom and Lazarus and the client 'Kathy', were well used in counselling training. Raymond Corsini tried a similar comparison in print, in the book *Five Therapists and a Client* (F.E. Peacock Publishing, Itasca, IL, 1991), although in our opinion his book is marred by several weaknesses. In the first place, the client is a fictional case, and the first session therefore written entirely from Corsini's imagination – drawing presumably on clients he has known. Second, there are inconsistencies even within the first session, making the case less plausible. Third, each of the responding therapists is asked to imagine how the therapy would go, similarly writing their own dialogue. This gives them *carte blanche* to develop the case along the lines they want their therapy to pursue, which demonstrates the validity of their approach, and in each case ends up with success for their method with the client.

We wanted to approach the question of how different therapists might work with the same client from yet another angle. We wanted a real client, not a fictional situation as in Corsini's work, but more perhaps as Gloria and Kathy were in the sessions recorded

with Rogers and other therapists. In this series, we wanted to pre-
serve ·the anonymity of the client, which a video or film cannot
do. We also wanted to avoid what we believe inevitably happened
in *Three Approaches to Psychotherapy*. The client is seen by three
therapists in turn, but may be influenced in her responses to the
second and third by what has happened in previous interview(s).
We wanted all the therapists to start with precisely the same information, and to see how they might take it from there. In this introduction, we explain how we went about that and subsequent parts
of the task.

Finding the clients

We used various contacts throughout the country to identify potential participants in the project, providing an outline of the method
to be used. We invited applications from people who had never
been in therapy before, since we wanted to avoid the contamination
of their material by what might otherwise have been influenced
from a previous therapist's interpretations. As it turned out, we
learned rather late in the day that one of the clients had had a very
short period of counselling with a person-centred counsellor, but
over a rather different presenting issue to the one she brought to her
first session with us.

After meeting those who were interested, and explaining to them
the method and the safety features which we describe in more detail
below, we invited them to return a consent form if they wished to
continue. Their consent did not bind them to final agreement to take
part, until the point at which they agreed to release the material
from the first session. They could withdraw at any moment up to
that point at which the therapists would receive their material, and
were therefore committed to work on it. We, for our part, promised
absolute confidentiality and anonymity (not even the publishers
would know their names and addresses), and control by the client
over any material which could lead to identification. We also asked
the clients to accept that we could not take them on for therapy,
and that we could not be held responsible for their therapy, although
we would endeavour to find them the most appropriate therapy
if, during the course of our contact with them throughout the project, they so desired it. We also made it clear that we might not use
their material, since we would be seeing more people than the series
could use.

Several potential candidates dropped out at this stage. Seven people responded that they wished to participate, and between us we arranged to meet those who agreed to take part for an initial interview. We arranged to meet for up to an hour, recording the interview. We told them as we started that we would say very little, except to prompt them to say a little more where we felt they might value such a response. Some were more fluent than others, but we hope that we did not over-influence the course of the interviews. It was to be the client's agenda which each presented to us, and through us, to their six therapists. Our own interventions are recorded word for word in the record of the first session.

Of the seven interviews, three proved unsuitable for use in the project. All three were as interesting as those we finally chose, but two of them proved too similar as presenting issues to another which we already hoped to use. The third interview concerned us both because of the age of the client, and also because our understanding of the material concerned us. We felt it wiser to leave the client with natural defences. We had to be as sure as we could be from one nondirected interview that our client would survive any of the stresses that might arise in the course of such a project.

We finished with four tapes from which to work, and we checked with the four clients that they still wanted to proceed before we transcribed the tapes. The second chapter of each volume in the series is a word-for-word transcript of the first interview. The only changes that have been made are to certain possible identifying features. These have been altered with the agreement and with the assistance of the client. The alterations made were internally consistent with the client's presenting story.

Once the transcript was prepared, it was sent to the client to be checked, particularly with regard to any further alterations necessary to disguise actual identity. We did not allow the client to change his or her mind about what had been said, unless to facilitate a disguise of identity, or where there was a clear typing error. Once more we made it clear that the client could withdraw from the project if he or she wished to. Only if the client was completely satisfied with the account to be sent to the therapists, and which would form the key chapter of the book, was the client then asked to assign the copyright of the material to the editors.

Finding therapists

Simultaneously, we started to look for therapists who could represent, at least in their theoretical position, the different approaches we wished to include in each volume. We wanted to find distinct methods or schools for each client, and where possible to have three male and three female therapists. Taking the four initial books in the series together, we hoped to represent every major school of therapy. Suggestions were gathered from our own contacts, and therapists who were unable to accept an invitation were asked to suggest a colleague who might. In some cases, we asked a professional society to nominate one of its members.

For the most part our task went smoothly enough, and the response we had was encouraging. Many of those who accepted our invitation quite rightly had one major reservation, that their work with clients depended partly (or in some cases largely) upon the face-to-face relationship, and working with its nuances. They accepted that in this case it was impossible to have that particularly subjective experience informing their work, although some more directly than others asked for our own observations, feelings and intuition in some of the questions they asked of us. This concern – a lack of direct contact with the client – was also given as the reason why some of those we approached to represent psychoanalytic psychotherapy in the *Charlie* volume turned down our invitation. This was the most difficult space to fill, although other reasons were also given, each one genuine in its own way. We began to wonder whether there was some resistance from therapists in this orientation to 'going public'. But perhaps it was pure coincidence that we had no such problems with any of the other therapies, including other psychodynamic and psychoanalytic approaches. We occasionally had a refusal, but nearly always with the suggestion of someone else we might ask, who then accepted.

Responding to the client

Our therapists were told, in the original invitation, that having read the material they would have the opportunity to ask further questions of the client, through us the editors. We felt that it would be disruptive for the client to meet each of the six therapists in turn, and that it would make the chances of identification rather greater, since it has remained the case that only the editors know who the clients really are. We were also concerned that we should continue to monitor what was happening for the client in the whole process. This is a person's life and story that we all have responsibility for, and while we wished the therapists to be totally honest, we also wished to ensure the clients survived, without unnecessary damage to them.

The therapists were therefore invited to ask for further information in order to address the headings we had suggested to them for their chapters to be consistent with one another. We all recognized, on both sides, that therapists would not bluntly ask questions of a client, but that some would take a life history early on, while others would expect such information to emerge during the course of therapy. We had to assume that there was certain information each therapist would hope to receive before the end of therapy. We were unprepared for just how much the therapists wanted to ask, and what we had thought would be a simple second interview proved to be more arduous and searching than either we or the clients could have imagined.

Most of the therapists sent long lists of areas they wished to explore further. Some sent questionnaires or psychometric tests. They asked in some cases for drawings, or for our own personal responses to the client. We collated the sets of questions so that they could be asked in a more or less natural sequence, putting questions from different therapists about particular aspects of the client's life or history in the same section of the interview, or where they were nearly identical asking them together. Although the therapists only received back the information for which they had clearly asked, where questions were almost the same they received the same material and a reprint of the other therapist's question. Similar areas were addressed, but very few questions were actually close enough to be asked together. In a few instances, where the client referred back to an answer already given to one therapist, we supplied that information as necessary to a second therapist whose question had evoked this reference.

The interviews with our clients at this stage took several hours – we met at least twice, in two cases three times, and in Jitendra's case four times. We carefully monitored how much the client could take, and asked periodically how much more they wanted to answer at that session. The questions were often searching and they sometimes gave rise to painful feelings and uncomfortable memories, although our experience was that none of the clients found this anti-therapeutic. They and we were stretched more than we might have anticipated, and we valued the immense thoughtfulness which the therapists had put into their questions, and the clients put into their answers.

Inevitably, there was a long gap between the first interview and this subsequent series of separate interviews, which took place much closer together. The original problems may have shifted a little, sometimes being slightly less troubling, sometimes slightly more so. The time lapse did not otherwise have much significance, except in the thought which each client had given to their own original material in the intervening period. Their own silent working on this material probably made their responses to the questions rather more full. Certainly many thousands of words were transcribed in each case, once again for the agreement of the client, before being sent off to the individual therapists. In all but one instance the client was seen by the same person throughout. In Morag's case, her original interview was with Michael Jacobs. To share the task of editing the four client volumes, it was necessary for her to be allocated to Moira Walker for the second and subsequent interviews and collation of material.

The therapists' task

The therapists' brief was to use the original material and supplementary information which they received from their questions and other 'tests' or questionnaires, to write an assessment of the client along the following lines, which form the main headings of each chapter.

1 A brief description of their own training background, and their therapeutic approach. Even though they are known to represent particular orientations (e.g. person-centred), we recognize that each therapist has particular ways of working, which might draw upon aspects of other approaches. What is important is to see how an actual therapist rather than a theoretical therapy works in practice.
2 The second section consists of the further questions which the therapist asked of the client through the editor therapist, and the responses they feel are relevant to their understanding of the client. Phrases such as 'When I met the client' refer to meeting the client via the editor. For reasons that have been explained already, none of the therapists made contact with or spoke directly to the clients.
3 The therapist's assessment of and reaction to the client – how he or she understands the client and the material the client has presented. This takes different forms, in line with the particular therapeutic approach, empathic identification with the client, counter-transference towards the client, etc. The therapists have been asked to provide indications or evidence of how they arrived at any formulation they might make, even if this is inevitably somewhat speculative.

4 The next section outlines therapeutic possibilities – indications and contraindications in the client and in the therapist/therapy, in that it may or may not be helpful for that particular client.
5 The fifth section hypothesizes the course of therapy – what form it might take, the methods, the contract, the theoretical approach in practice, and any shifts in approach that might be necessary to accommodate the particular client.
6 Next, the therapist suggests possible problem areas and how they might be resolved. We have asked that potential difficulties are faced and not given a favourable gloss if it seems the client might not prove amenable to some aspects of a particular approach.
7 The therapist is asked to explain his or her criteria for success in this case and to try to predict how far these may be met. Aware of the positive outcome in all Corsini's therapists' accounts, we asked the therapists not to predict a totally positive outcome if they had any doubts about it.
8 Each therapist concludes with a short summary and a short reading list for those interested in pursuing his or her approach.

The final stage

As the therapists returned their assessments of the client, and their accounts of how they would work with him or her, the material was passed over to the client to read. When all six assessments had been received, we met with the client for a penultimate session, to discuss the content of the final chapter together, before the editor wrote it. While it had been generally obvious throughout just how much the clients had gained from the process, their own final assessment both of the therapists and of the process is therefore available at the end of each book. We intend to meet with them one more time, when the book is published, to complete our part in their own search for change and understanding.

To them and to the therapists who took part we owe a great debt. They have each in their own way demonstrated a deep commitment to each other, and have furnished the reader with a unique opportunity of comparing not only their own approaches, but also the reader's response to the client with their own. (Following the client's original story in Chapter 2, the reader will find space in Chapter 3 to record ideas, questions and feelings with headings that are similar to those questions we asked each therapist.) The therapists have also shown a willingness to work cooperatively in a project which will do much to advance the comparative study of the many different approaches and nuances which the psychotherapy and counselling world embraces. This series shows how little need there is for competition, and how the different therapies can complement one another in the service of those who seek their help.

2 JITENDRA

LOST CONNECTIONS

Jitendra, or more familiarly Jitu, is in his early forties. He is a consultant psychiatrist, enquiring about the possibility of therapy for himself. He is medium to tall, slimly built, bearded and well groomed, and he is wearing a dark suit. He has had periods when he has very much wanted help in trying to cope with vulnerable times, although currently he is, as he says when he starts, 'relatively OK'. He speaks sometimes with care, measured in his expression. At other times he speaks quickly, with a flowing picture in particular of his childhood and later memories. There are occasional long pauses, where it feels as if much more than a prompt is necessary to help him to resume. It is in fact very difficult to keep more incisive interventions out of the interview (and as the chapter shows, I cannot avoid the occasional comment of this type), although I remain conscious throughout of not wanting to steer him in a particular direction. I sense a wish in him for me to connect in some clear way to what he is saying if he is to be able to continue during this interview.

It's difficult to say anything at this point of time, partly because one's feeling relatively OK, but there have been times when things have been more depressing, where one can talk about that fairly clearly and with meaning. And these are linked with other problems. But I should like to see a therapist for two broad categories: one is from a personal point of view, as a private individual, to understand myself; and also as somebody who is looking after other human beings. I realize that essentially it is understanding myself, but only in understanding myself may I understand other people. So there is a two-pronged approach. And there is a sort of related theme, which is that of seeking meaning in life, which I think can be linked to either of those areas.

In terms of my personal life, I think one thing that sort of interests me and sometimes worries me is my early years, my childhood years.

I have very few memories of anything before the age of six or five, but I am sure that they have left some legacy behind, a significant legacy, and sometimes I have deep feelings of sadness or complexity or ambivalence which are not immediately ascribable to events happening around me. And I wonder what these . . . what this augurs. I think a therapist might sort of help me in this area. The other area that I am wanting to understand is the dynamics of a large extended family. I am the middle of five sons. I also have two sisters, and so we were quite a large family, and there was quite an extended family of my father's brothers and a sister; and the extended family is still very much part of my life. I would like to understand a little bit more about what affects a person's growing up in that context.

A central event in my life is the death of my father when I was ten. I think I get glimpses and remember grieving at his loss, but I think essentially the process has been blocked out. I believe that. I think this is something that I feel is very important in my life, particularly now, as I'm a father myself; and this was more apparent two years ago when my daughter was ten. I think at this time it was very important. I think I should like to understand that.

Much more recently is when I came to this country – I was eighteen – and how the transition, how if you like as I was at eighteen – and that was possibly related to my early childhood and also to events happening at that time – how this complete person, this person at that stage, responded to the change of moving from Uganda to here; and again I do not think that I actually worked with the process; I think I focused on adapting, rather than working through the process of adapting, and I feel that is unfinished business with me. I wouldn't mind working at it. I've been working at it for a few years now. But on my own. I believe that another person would help very much.

Then, moving on from then . . . I think . . . I'm married to a white girl, an Irish girl, and this has brought to the surface for me the issue of culture. Not so much in the early years of the marriage, but certainly after about seven or eight years of marriage – I've now been married for about twelve years. The issue of culture, and how it affects experience. And this becomes very important, I think, when there are children involved in a relationship, especially when one has to choose about transmitting cultures to children; there culture becomes much more an explicit issue. It has led to a lot of problems I think for me and for my relationship with my wife, the idea of culture. And the related issue is one of religion, which is linked to culture, but can be quite independent of it. I am of a Hindu background, and my wife comes from a Protestant background. And this has been an area of . . . certainly [*Jitu hesitates*] . . . of personal conflict and suffering, I would say, directly with my wife, and indirectly in relation to the children, and what one should tell them about how one should view the world.

This leads on to the wider problem of living in a culture which, in a way, is historically unrelated to the culture one originates from, although I must emphasize that this process was not new to us in East Africa, because we had left . . . my father had left India twenty years before I was born; and in the same process we left Uganda for the UK so there is a lot of cultural – if you like – continuity, adaptation that is not new to us. But it is how one adapts to a different culture, and particularly a culture where, because one is in a minority, one seems not to be valued. But on the other hand, it is one's own country as well because at a particular moment in time you accept parts of it, and you go along with it in that society, but there is internally a division of the part that is adaptive and accepts a lot of things that are current, and the other part which feels unrecognized but which links up to the past. So these are the areas that I bring to therapy myself.

[*There comes the first of a number of pauses which feel like a full stop. I wonder where Jitu might want to take it from there, because there is time to begin thinking about anything he wants to.*]

I think there is a thing beyond it, and that is to do with . . . it is a deeper question of meaning, enlightenment or salvation, whatever: I don't know what is the right word. It's questioning what is real, really. It is real that you find yourself at a particular moment in time and space, to be born in a particular family, culture, religion, and so on. When you realize that other people are in a distinct situation, multiplied millions of times across the world, you realize it is a chance event. And when you attract to the other person there is awareness of difference, but I feel, and I believe that things must go beyond us, and if it is to do with spiritual realization – it's a vague intellectual idea, I haven't experienced it – there is a direction that I feel I am drawn to, that is directly related to what I have mentioned. And I would expect a therapist to perhaps tackle that at some stage. I would expect that sort of interaction. If it wasn't it would be a terrible . . . it would be a gap in the relationship for me.

In terms of choosing where to start [*Jitu pauses briefly*] . . . I think that depends on what is most pressing. I think the most relevant issue is the traversing . . . the middle stage of life, as I see it. It's a transitional phase for me and my development, and all the other issues I've mentioned are in danger of it, there is no doubt about that. There is actually a real experience of moving in a different phase, you know, of moving from a young man's stage to early middle age, these types of things I am very much aware of. And I think this is related to two things: mainly living, accepting, coping with one's limitations or imperfections, loss of achievements; perhaps coming to terms with mortality or death is, I think, central.

[*I comment that these* sound *as if they are intellectual, but that I feel that they are not intellectual.*]

No, they are not. It's a sense of meaninglessness . . . there is a part of me that feels a sense of meaninglessness at times, a certain sense of confusion, a lack of direction if I may say so; a lack of flow, I think, somehow a lack of connectedness: these are the essential feelings. Yes. The other thing at a practical level is being reminded of illness and death in people who are one's contemporaries, or certainly in people of one's parents' age. One is expected to look after them in that situation not only as a professional but as a person. One can't but link to it at a personal level. And that level is not direct, but I think there is deep down . . . These feelings which well up, I think, are related to these themes. I'm sure of that. [*There is a brief silence.*]

Another central theme is coming to terms with contradictions and polarities not only external to oneself, but also inside oneself: the awareness that one mustn't be too divisive, one must not project things, and split things outside of oneself. Say that other people are violent and not be aware of one's own violence. I feel this is terrible to come to terms with, it disconnects and doesn't fit. You can feel the tearing apart of the polarities in yourself at times. I see this as an issue too.

[*Jitu is still hesitantly, though thoughtfully, moving around different areas. It feels important to make a more definite response, which I try to resist, not wanting to direct the interview. I decide to try and repeat the areas he has so far mentioned, but I cannot avoid linking them – connecting in fact – all these around the issue of 'connection': that Jitu would like to connect to his early years, to the time of his father's death, to the transition from Uganda to here, to issues to do with his wife and family and culture, and to parts of himself. At each of these subjects he says 'Yes', and nods. I then wonder which of these would feel most appropriate to take forward at the moment.*]

I think the theme of my relationship with my father and his death would link up with the preoccupation with death. It's a very good starting point which would lead into other issues. So it is the theme of dying, I think. I think what I would like to have an experience of now . . . is to get some idea of me as a little boy and the relationship with my father, and of course my parents and my brothers; but I think it was my father's death that was instrumental in extinguishing, putting a block on these processes.

I had a really warm relationship with my father, as far as I can remember. Some of the images I have are of evening time, when he was at home; my brothers are doing homework, and him coming in from work; and going to my father's room; and he was very fond of getting into his night-clothes, and just sitting on his bed either phoning people, or just sitting with him talking, in a very jocular way about things. I can see the way. I can't remember the content of the things, but I think we were sort of valued and loved. But at the same time, one part of him wanted to and liked to tussle with you, and I can remember sitting, trying to outwit him, but he would always be one step ahead. And I can remember my mother sitting on the side of the bed, and I can remember that as a loving memory. The other image I have of him is when he became ill. He became ill a couple of years before he died. That image is one of him struggling upstairs; he was a short stocky man, but very physically vigorous, full of energy, and quite an extrovert, a very liked person in the community. I used to see him coming up the stairs, when I was eight or nine – I think that it upset me terribly. There were concrete stairs. I can still see him coming, struggling, in his suit, short of breath, always short of breath. I think that affected me.

And then the next image is one of him becoming very ill. Although I think it was a big, large family, as children we were used to having an intimate relationship of the type where you exchange thoughts and feelings on a daily basis. When you needed a parent you went to them. I knew he wasn't well, because although we weren't told it, we guessed at it, picked up word. He had to go to Kampala and see a specialist. And then he stayed in Kampala. Him going away for short periods was not unusual for us. It was common in the family in the school holiday – one of us went away to stay with cousins for weeks on end. If he went away it was more unusual. Then suddenly hearing that he was very seriously ill, and he had deteriorated. And then being brought back by ambulance. I wasn't there when the ambulance came to our house. In actual fact I came back from school and then, the following morning, my mother said to come and give him his last rites. We usually offer milk or holy water to people who are dying, and all the children had to do that. And I remember that very much.

And I gave him milk and holy water, and told him to have a 'safe journey'. And afterwards I remember, if you like, missing him for a long time. I think that lasted about two or three years. At that time I was twelve or thirteen, and I think I have, somehow – although I don't have actual experience of it – I subliminated my experience into working hard at school. And I think it was a process whereby I was doing very well at school and I was getting a lot of attention, and a lot of recognizing my needs to be cared for that way, I think. And I have had opportunities later on of reviving it, but somehow I've never taken it up. Other things have been preoccupying me.

My brother-in-law died last year. And now I hear of people dying like at my stage of life, or my uncles, both my uncles – two of my father's brothers – died in the last five years. Although it's something I read about it's not something that's easy to talk about, to be honest. I haven't spoken about these things as much as I have done today. I think just having the vignettes, and the images associated with them, and feeling the feelings for the boy I was then – I think that's very hard. I felt very intensely at that time. But talking like this now, it is not as lively as I would like it to be. There is a little bit of fear in me as to what would happen. The other thing is you wonder how much you have blocked out, blocked against oneself. It is, I would say, a tragedy for my own life. I think since the age of ten I have not really dealt with feelings. I have to act a certain role . . . sort of . . . I feel there are restrictions.

I think the relationship with my mother is very important as well. She had a large family to support. I can remember her the day after my father died: my mother waking up, doing everything in the house. Breakfast was ready; she made phone calls to many people; at lunchtime I can see her sitting downstairs. And my auntie, my uncle's, my father's brother's wife, telling her to behave herself, because my mother was breaking down. One thing that is very good for me living in Birmingham is that all my brothers live here, and we relate very well with each other; most of us talk to each other quite intimately about virtually all things, although we haven't quite approached the subject directly, but we talk fairly openly. I feel much more sorry for my sister, who was only two when my father died. She is a very capable young woman with a family of her own and with a very good job. She's a wonderful person; she holds the family together; and we talk to each other many times a week. I sometimes wonder what happened to her when I know what happened to me. She was even smaller than me.

So if you like we're collectively responsible for it. It's not just yourself. We talk of here and now, of how the relationships in the family are *now*. That's very explicit, very intimate. There is always a support; but I do think my father's death is like a shadow over us. I'm sure of that. It is like talking about something you can't even see, if you see what I mean.

One event that I do remember was fairly recent. In these societies, and in my family, we have rites for the dead which go on for several days after the death of the person, and then at three-monthly intervals, six-monthly intervals, yearly intervals. My mother still calls us for a remembrance ceremony every year. My mother has faced a lot in our family. My brother Harish – he died, at the age of forty. He was very cultured, very good looking. It was difficult for him, coming to this country, getting qualifications, but nevertheless he adjusted to that. It was no problem.

My mother has never recovered from that. He was the eldest son. We had five years ago a big ceremony for both of them, and I remember it went on for seven days; and a priest would talk about him, and I remember for the first time all the family being there. The priest was rather a strange character but he talked of my father and brother. And I think it was a really moving experience for me. I remember crying. It reminded me of that earlier time. My second brother Arvint is a very strong person, but when my brother died and with all these ceremonies, I'd never seen him cry. I suddenly saw him cry. His crying upset me more, although indirectly. It wasn't only my brother Harish. I can still see his face, coming out of the house, the coffin and the car, and I turned round and I saw Arvint my brother and it was sort of suffering personified – that was very upsetting. I think it does affect me very much in my professional life in the sense of how I deal with grief. I don't know whether one can help somebody who has a problem similar to one's own and one has not worked through that. I don't know. But certainly whatever blind spots or blanks I may have, I imagine it affects them. They've not told me that, but I expect that. I imagine that's how it is.

[*This is another point where the interview stops. I comment that Jitu has described how he would like to get in touch with his feelings, and that he is aware of a difficulty in doing that and achieving that. I wonder if this is part of his culture, although he has said that his brothers are capable of showing a lot of feeling. I ask if there is something else that holds Jitu back.*]

I think it's firstly personal, in that it is my will to negate emotion. I think it may be cultural as well, but I don't think it is that important. I think most of it is about the way I chose to deal with it; and being a male and the gender bit is I think important. I think that my brothers are similar to me, though I think that other men are similar to me as well, so I don't feel that there is a difference. I think one way it shows in me as a person, unlike all my brothers, is that I'm over-intellectualized. I am aware of that. I realize it is a defence of some sort. That may link up with my relationship with my father. I always had a closer relationship with him than any of my brothers, or so I've been told. My relationship with him was different. I think I was his favourite son, which is surprising because I was the middle son; usually it is the eldest. Yes, certainly I was his favourite. Although I like to think that all my brothers were treated equally. I haven't talked to them about this – they just tell me that I was his favourite and they remember that.

The issue of culture somewhat impinges on this. I think it is to do with separation: how people separate themselves through culture. I've found this very much with my relationship with my wife and my friends. And I try to link it up to my personal experience, and not just as cultural, although I think the issue of culture does link to you as a person. I think it's the issue of separation.

[*Jitu pauses. I observe that he has said he is separate from his wife and friends, but there is also something about being separate from his brothers too*.]

Yes. One part of me is a loner really. It is true. Although I superficially give the impression of relating and connecting with people, I think one part of me is very much private. I have always been aware of my separateness from everybody. I am also guarded actually. If I'm ever in a group, I don't get too identified with that group. I will never exclusively relate to a particular person. I always try and keep myself away from a central position [*he pauses*].

I think it may be something to do with being overwhelmed by the present in a sense, although I do not know what present I am talking about or where this comes from. There is a sense of one part in me observing my other part. I think that is why I can be withdrawn. I know that is there. I've always chosen to do things differently from the family. As I say, I married an Irish girl. All the other brothers, although they too went to university and studied, came back. I always chose to be different. But I don't think that I was merely reacting to something. That I too made the choices. I've chosen these things.

This was quite apparent to me when I went back to India recently. I was quite happy to be myself and different from the relatives in the village or India generally as a country. I felt I was different and separate and also glad to be that. That connects with the separateness. I made connections, but not of the type I fantasized about. I went to different places. I acknowledged where I had something in common, but also that I was separate and different; and I felt good about it.

I think being different can relate to early childhood. One of the stories I do remember is when I was a little boy I was very fond of an African woman, who lived . . . I don't remember, but my brothers told me, that I would stay with her sometimes for a whole day, and she was so fond of me that she treated me like a mother. And I would eat with her and everything. But I have no memory of this woman. I know the name, I remember how she was related . . . We had a servant and it was his wife. They lived just across the courtyard. She cared for me, I think. I think my mother in no way did not care for me. I'm sure of that. But I feel this may be something to do with it. I had a different early upbringing, if you like. Different from my family. And I have always had an affinity with African people, which my mother has not understood. Where I was at school I had friends from every sort of background, and they were all treated the same in my home, more or less. They all would come to my house. I think my mother was horrified that I would mix with Africans. She never *said* it to me; and I must say that was sort of nice, you know, in a family, that people were allowed to be themselves. There was a certain type of behaviour, which was not overruled by individual feelings; and I still feel good about that. I remember they were all treated the same.

[*Jitu pauses. After a brief silence I say, 'You like to be different. And also connected'.*]

It's how I am, I suppose. Do I like that part of me? Yes, although at times it can be a handicap, in an extended community where you are expected to conform. Since coming back to Birmingham I have actually very much become part of the family network, where I wasn't at one stage, when I went to university. I have come back into the fold, and there's a large degree of freedom associated with it, so I feel OK now. I know where my limits might lie.

[*There is another full stop. I break the awkward blankness by saying that he has said that at certain times he clearly wants help. At present he seems on a type of plateau. It is not that everything is straightforward, but it appears as if he is saying that nothing troubles him that much that he feels impelled to be in therapy. Jitu thinks about this for a short while.*]

I think that's true at this moment in time. I think when suffering is acute the need for understanding, for clarity, for support is very great.

[*He pauses. I say, 'But you also at other times want to be more distant'.*]

I think my presence would not be there very much and I might even degenerate into playing games. I think it would be the therapist's task to keep me in balance. But now you've pointed it out, I would guard myself against doing that. It is a way of coping, I am sure of that. But deep down there is the other bit of 'what is the point of bringing these things out?' Although you know it somehow, that they do connect, they are relevant, the realization is not so intense that you need to follow it through. There is a sense of starting from here and now, if you like. You know: 'Today is the first day of your life'. I know that sounds trite but it's not. The past is relevant, but also realizing the limitations of its relevance. The future is connected to the past but . . . [*Jitu pauses*] . . . not so tightly that the past is to be explicitly clear, or reaches towards the future.

I think it's also to do with centring yourself, in terms of thinking, of feeling or, one can say, the spiritual side. Trying to put oneself in the psychological state of being in connection. [*He pauses again.*] There's large doubt and uncertainty about it. Although in one sense its defensive, I think to me as a person the ethical dimension is very important in life – not only in my work but in life generally. By 'ethical' I mean it's to do with a certain order if you like, with what is right or good behaviour, with good thinking or right thinking, with *dharma*: I think it's to do with not harming, for example, or not being violent, on one level, though there are issues about violence; the thing about being truthful and seeking truth. I am not sure how the past, the history, relates to truth, that whole issue, as I see it. I am not very clear about these ideas. These are ideas that appeal to me. I see that as very important in my life.

[*Again a stop. I felt like bringing the interview to an end, and I hold back because I am anxious not to lead; but again it is very difficult for Jitu to go on without some kind of clear response. What I say is that I have a feeling I would have to be a bit more violent with him to get him to open up.*]

'You're right. Yes'. [*I then observe that there is a protectiveness about him, which is very important for him, but keeps me away.*]

Yes. I think that's right. I think it might be an imperative of the therapist that they do that to me. I think it would be perfectly necessary for me. I think I would feel vulnerable, and I think for me to be vulnerable is a very hard state to be. I have had that experience. I think it's a difficult way of living and I'm not sure how much I can cope with it, to be honest. Maybe I need to be violent with myself. And maybe the violence is to be expressed against my father as well. Or against fate. Certainly I have a lot of anger and rage, which does become manifest at times.

My deeper interest in therapy and in my own work did arise at a time when I was very vulnerable. Absolutely. I'm sure that's true. I felt vulnerable when my previous programmes or attitudes or relationships weren't working and new problems came in. It was new to me. It was very strange to think that way.

I think there has been some violence I have used against myself ... [*he pauses*] ... namely, going back and finding out to what extent I have been in ways, and traits ... I realize until I was eighteen I lived essentially an Indian life. And this came out to the fore when I was in India recently. People couldn't believe that I am from England, that I was from the big cities, that I spoke the language; my behaviour, the whole thing was exactly as they were used to. But I think I'm also quite good at relating to English people actually. That it's like wearing clothes. That was a very nice pleasant discovery, exposure to the experience, so I've come back really valuing the difference, if you like.

3 THE READER'S
RESPONSE

Before reading further, the reader is given space to record a personal response to the client, and to questions similar to those which the six therapists were asked to address.

What does this client make you feel?

How might you use what you feel in understanding and working with this client?

What more do you want to know? Is there any information which is crucial at this stage?

Thus far, how do you understand this client and the material the client has presented?

What indications are there so far in this client that lead you to feel that you could work with him?

What contraindications are there?

What, if any, will be your focus?

What will be your method, as related to this client?

What difficulties do you anticipate you might encounter?

What in your view might be a favourable outcome for this client?

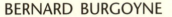

4 BERNARD BURGOYNE

LACANIAN PSYCHOANALYSIS

The therapist

In England, what it means to be a psychoanalyst needs constantly reiterating: there is not a widespread understanding of the nature of analytical work, of its aims, or of the means that it uses to achieve these ends. This was not how things were up to the period immediately after the Second World War. But at some point during the 1950s, the formulations produced in Britain concerning the nature of psychoanalysis began to lose touch completely with the reality of psychoanalysis as it was practised on the continent of Europe, and as it is now practised throughout the world. Within large parts of the International Psychoanalytical Association, which counts as members about half the psychoanalysts in the world, and of which the established British tradition forms a component part, the views of the British Psycho-Analytic Society are seen as somewhat conservative and inadequate as a proposed version of the contemporary situation and content of psychoanalysis. And as for the ten thousand or so Lacanian psychoanalysts whose work has almost never been referred to over the past forty years in Anglo-Saxon psychoanalytical literature, their schools have produced an immense amount of research and articulation within the field of psychoanalysis, and one can rely on the fact that these developments remain largely unknown in this country. This situation demands some remedy. Psychoanalysis is a response to human suffering, a form of intervention in human suffering that operates entirely through the medium of words. It is one of the central theoretical problems of psychoanalytical work to explain how it is that the speaking and listening that constitute the analytical situation operate so as to bring into being a different relation to that suffering: How it is that a talking cure can cause a change in a person's life, and allow that person new options as to how they can act?

In the 1970s, it seemed that very little analytical work in Britain did anything other than issue standardized recipes for this work, and it seemed that this tradition of work had lost sight of analytical prospects and problems as they had been introduced and developed by Freud. It was against the background of these realities, then, that I was led to question what psychoanalysis had to offer in addressing questions of human reason and pain, and to compare it with other attempts to locate and resolve questions of irrationality and repetitive forms of suffering in everyday life. Two things seemed fairly clear to me twenty years ago: the first was that Freud had discovered and formulated a whole range of powerful themes and modes of intervention that allowed the prospect of shifts to be brought about in the everyday realities of human misery; the second was that work on the problems and difficulties of this psychoanalytic way of addressing human relationships was being developed and furthered only in some schools of psychoanalysis. And it was not in this country that the work was being done, but in the schools set up or influenced by Jacques Lacan. I visited Paris to follow Lacan's seminars throughout 1977 and 1978, and it soon became evident that the view from the other side (of the Channel) provided a prospect for tackling and resolving the central and classical problems of psychoanalysis, and for giving cogency to the analytical enterprise. My work with Lacan's school in the 1970s and 1980s led me to respond to the state of things in England by collaborating in the founding in 1985 of what is now the Centre for Freudian Analysis and Research in London.

This school trains psychoanalysts, and provides a regular and public programme of seminars and lectures that seeks to present the concepts and problems in Freud's work from the perspective of Lacan. Lacan had claimed that his work could be seen as a working through of the problems addressed by Freud, and in fact this claim to be the legitimate inheritor of Freud's work explains some of the bitterness of his conflict with the Anglo-Saxon schools. Such a 'return' to Freud needs to be presented at the start of Jitendra's case, because nothing in the existing analytical literature in the Anglo-Saxon tradition allows the assumption that these basic themes in Freud can be taken as known.

The central theme in psychoanalysis is the Oedipus Complex. This Oedipal history is a story of how a child fights desperately and dramatically to protect its first love relation against the challenges to it. The reconstruction of this warfare is at the heart of psychoanalytical work: there are schools – important schools – which want to discount the centrality of this complex, but for Freud the entire cloth of unconscious representations is woven from the fabric of the Oedipal struggle. The mother's involvement with someone other than the child produces the third point for this love triangle – a person intervening in the child's world fulfilling the 'function' of the father. This struggle of love is negotiated by the child in terms that the adults already use to represent their world and their desires. In the process of this fight, the child inherits phantasies and desires, and maintains a structure of unfinished and broken love relations as the kernel of his unconscious representations of the world, and of his relations to others. The words for these loves are beyond Jitendra; it is the task for the analysis to regain access to a world which, since Jitendra's childhood, has been lost to him. The British schools say that the words are not the most important thing; the Lacanian schools claim that all else depends on them.

Initial assessment

My first impressions of Jitendra are of a man who distances himself from feeling, weaving a world rather of thinking, knowing and doubting.

His presenting symptoms form two strata: at the centre of them are two precise problems, that of his not having 'dealt with feelings' since his father's death, and the difficulties he expresses of being part of a large family – like that of his father. Surrounding these problems with the father there are very generally expressed and more diffuse difficulties: with his marriage, problems of cultural difference, and of his relation to the past. There are connecting links in the material that Jitendra produces: some of them he is aware of, many of them he is not. The analysis of Jitendra's history, of the way that it constructs and determines his present, starts by listening for these links, and bringing the crucial one to Jitendra's attention.

Jitendra tells a story of his love for his mother, and his love for an African woman who in some ways stood in for her. He does not say 'love': for the African woman he says, 'I was very fond of [her]', and for his mother, '[her] care for me'. He uses the same word, 'care', for the African woman when he compares the two women in a passage where he tries to present his early childhood and its loves. When he describes his relation to his mother he uses a double negative: she 'in no way did not care for me'. And the phrase with which he surrounds this is: 'I think ... I'm sure of that'. Not only do these phrases refer directly to the mass of 'I think's' that occur at the start of his presentation of himself, but the 'I think' leads to a structure of repressions and symptoms that have marked out and hindered Jitendra's life since these early years. 'I'm sure' occurs in another place in his account of his history, at the point where he gives a very generalized account of his feelings and confusions: 'illness and death in people who are one's contemporaries, or certainly in people of one's parents' age'. This veiled reference to his father's death ends with: 'These feelings . . . I think, are related to these themes, I'm sure . . .'.

When he talks about love for his mother, it is in connection with his father's death. His mother had sat 'on one side' of his father's bed, Jitendra on another side: 'I can remember that', he says, 'as a loving memory'. The history he tells is of a 'really warm relationship' with the father, and of this 'loving memory' of the mother with the father and himself; but it immediately gives way to an account of his father's illness and death. The 'warm' relation to the father is qualified: 'as far as I can remember', Jitendra adds. It is wanting to remember what he cannot at the moment remember that has brought him to therapy: the legacy of his 'early years, my childhood years' are, he says, a 'significant legacy . . . I am sure'. There is a complex here, connecting love for the mother and his father's death. Jitendra had to wait two years for his father's death, after the first signs of his illness had appeared; he waited two years before seeking a therapist, after experiencing the feelings of having a child reach the age that he was when his father died.

Jitendra takes therapeutic work, probing the relation of the past to the present, to have to do with 'centring yourself'. Earlier he described his father's death as a central event in his life. He says, in terms of keeping himself distant from individuals in groups: 'I always try and keep myself away from a central position'. I would attempt an interpretation of this material, even in a preliminary interview, saying something of the form: 'although you are at the centre of five sons'. This interpretation introduces an equivocation, and is intended to do so: its aim is to keep terms, which Jitendra assumes have nothing to do with his family complex, linked to it. Wherever there is a reference to a centre in Jitendra's speech, there is an allusion to the father complex.

These warm and loving relations with the father and the mother are presented in a scene that he has little difficulty in remembering. In contrast, of the African woman he says, 'I have no memory of this woman'. He knows, he says, her name. I will ask for this name if he doesn't proffer it; and I want to follow the thread of the memories attached to it, more likely to lead to the complex of love relations to the mother than the profession of 'warmth' for the father. Jitendra also says his aim is to understand himself. I do not normally take someone on who really has this as their primary aim; many people say that it is, and it is quite clear that it is not. It is not in the case of Jitendra.

At the end of this preliminary interview, I intend to propose working with Jitendra, assuming him to have the structure of an obsessional neurosis. I will describe a little later some of the elements of this structure. The symptoms, rather than the structure, are what present themselves initially, and are less reliable as indicators. Quite simply, symptoms shift: a hysteric can have obsessional symptoms, and it can be that obsessional symptoms cover over the structure of a psychosis. From this first interview, and much more convincingly from the two that follow, the conclusion can be drawn that Jitendra is obsessional: there are a great number of obsessional traits in the material that he presents, and no indication of any psychotic phenomenon. The neurosis he displays has the following symptomatology: repeated displacements by generalization; fairly systematic doubt, with a corresponding search for what is sure; a longing for an imaginary world free of troubles; isolations and idealizations in what would otherwise be situations of satisfaction, rendering impossible any relationship that contains themes of sexual love; ambivalence in close relations, itself tied to the generalizing function.

In addition, there are occasional traits of hysteria. He twice mentions how terrible it is to have to face gaps and divisions within himself and in his relations to other people. That he has some awareness of these conflicts represents a move away from the obsessional structure, although he talks about them in very general contexts, and repeats the same word 'terrible' in each context. From the analytical point of view, finding any hysterical trait already present in the obsession is an advantage: Freud saw obsessional neurosis as a 'dialect' of hysteria, further removed than hysteria from the underlying realities of the conditions of human life.

The obsessional structure keeps Jitendra away from this. When he describes his brother's death, his phrases hide away the reality of it entirely – his brother, he says, had 'no problem'. Two others remind him of his distress: a brother and his mother. Overriding what he knows to be a region of 'blind spots' there is the insistent assumption that he is 'OK' and that he is in control: he 'chose' to negate his emotions. All these obsessional structures are strongly developed in Jitendra. Obsessionality is one of the two main structures of neurosis, and is very conducive for analytical work. There are less difficulties involved in working with obsessional neurosis than there are in working with phobias, perversions or psychosis. It is, however, lengthy work. The Lacanian aim in this work is to hysterisize the structure, so as to give more access to the divisions that constitute the kernel of the Oedipal relations. The aim then is to allow Jitendra to be more in contact with, and to become more able to tolerate, the underlying anxieties that at the moment he flees from.

Jitendra is clearly obsessional. I would take him on.

Further information requested

The further questions that I asked Jitendra took two sessions to discuss. They were made up of three series of questions. I wanted him to say something about his family background, and I started by asking about his mother, keeping his father absent for a while. I then asked him about his father's leaving, maintaining the father in an absent position. I then asked him about his father's parents, and about his father's difficulties in moving to Africa. I asked about his father's relations within his own family, and finally, in this first series of questions, about his father's relation with his mother. In asking these questions I was not looking for any actual series of influences that could be supposed to have constructed his current problems; rather, I was trying to find out how he constructs his history, and by allowing his associations to connect to this story, to discover in what ways this history has constructed him.

Jitendra's answers to these questions set up in a preliminary form the way that he represents the world that contains his love relation to his mother. He describes his father as having a subordinate position after the move away from his mother: 'he was really subject to the orders of his older brothers'; 'he had a tough life with that woman [a sister-in-law]'; '[in relation to his older brothers] he was subject to whatever they asked him to do'. After his father set up his own business, the situation was a little better: 'I could remember, he would buy clothes'. Jitendra had ended the original session with such a comment, that he found that he could 'relate well' to English people: 'it's like wearing clothes'. And he made this comment immediately after wondering whether or not he felt a lot of anger and violence against his father. Jitendra has probably not noticed a thread which connects clothes to hostility towards his father; it is the analyst's job to notice, and sometimes to convey this link to the analysand. Jitendra's father had left India 'in his teens or early twenties' – Jitendra himself had left Africa for England at about the same age. Jitendra recognizes the sexual level of the relation between his mother and father, but is unwilling immediately to talk about the relationship in terms of love: 'Did he court her? I think the relationship, if I speculate, was one of duty rather than love'. He had used such a phrase a little earlier when talking of his father not having a tenable place in the village in India: 'I am speculating now

. . . there was no future for him, if you like'. And there is in this a further redolence to: 'my mother was never not pregnant, if you like'. The double negative is the same form that he uses when he talks of his mother's love for him, contrasting it to his relation with the African woman. Jitendra talks about his father's mother, clearly remembering her love for him. And this love he felt: 'she was one of the few people I felt love from'. He says nothing of this woman's relation to his father: it is as though he has taken her love away from his father, taken it for himself. His father's father he never met, although, he says, he was a man of 'stature'.

He knows more about his mother's family, in particular about his mother's grandparents. His great-grandmother was a woman strong enough to ignore convention: '[she] was in fact living with a man'. There is no problem about the love relationship between these great-grandparents: 'For practical purposes they were man and wife'; '[he] decided to settle with her'. Unlike the hesitancy that Jitendra has with his father's love for his mother, the love bond here is unambiguous and clear. However, the great-grandmother 'was a matriarch in the real sense of the term, and she controlled the family'. His mother's family was poor, and when she left her family for her husband's, she 'was the wife of the youngest son . . . the lowest of the low'. Jitendra's grandfather in this family was not only successful, but also a heroin addict, so there are questions about *his* 'stature'. Jitendra's mother tells him that she would feed 'morsels of heroin' to his brother when 'he was demanding of her'. There was nothing unusual in this; it will be seen to connect, however, to Jitendra's own relation to his mother and to his 'other mother'. In her husband's family, his mother 'had to answer to the needs' of almost everyone, and it is in these circumstances, after she had suffered the death of a baby, that Jitendra's father chose to leave her, to go to Africa. Jitendra presents it not as a choice, but as a weakness of the father's position: 'he was I think virtually asked to go to [Africa]'; the absence was 'for many years'.

The power of words is at the heart of the psychoanalytical relation: the words that are active in this way are those used by the analysand, and not those introduced by the analyst. Such an action is at play in the phrase that Jitendra uses in describing his father's relation to his mother: his father had left the mother alone with the children 'for many years'. The redolence of this phrase allows it to stand alone as a term that pins down a moment of Jitendra's history: in the family myth into which Jitendra was born, his mother had been without her man, and a chasm between the mother and the father had been in existence even before Jitendra was born. Within such a complex of memories and ideas, Jitendra can imagine his father absent very easily. The leaving and the joining are part of a history he recalls in terms of the sexual link between the parents 'a lot of physical intimacy . . . my mother was never not pregnant, if you like'. So there is a prehistory, where the mother was always accessible without the father, and his actual childhood, where the father (apart from a number of excursions) was always present.

The memory that Jitendra produces of 'a lot' of sexual intimacy is produced by his hindsight. In terms of the experience of his childhood, there is a passage in his responses to my questions where his view of their separation seems to be central to his representation of their relationship: 'To talk of them in relationship terms as husband and wife . . . would be very difficult. I think, um, amongst Asian women . . . there is definitely a world between a husband's and a wife's world'. This is one of the first problems raised by our questioning and answering: Does Jitendra assume a reality to the sexual relations between the mother and the father, a reality that he could respond to with a challenge, or does he rather see the father as quiet, pacific, not asserting his sexual possession of the mother, and allowing Jitendra the prospect of a peaceable possession of an idyllic mother? It is this second alternative that sets a predisposing scenario for an obsessional neurosis.

The obsessional has a particular strategy, with respect to his relation to the mother. The first step of this plan for unconscious desire is the idealization of the mother. This is part of an attempt to calm the Oedipal conflicts, by a pretence that there is no need for conflict of any kind. The mother is out of the sexual conflict, and the father correspondingly has nothing to fight for. There is very much of this with Jitendra, all of it supported by a mother who actually struggled fairly heroically in very difficult circumstances to bring up her children:

> She was the wife of the youngest son when she married my father . . . she got married when she was very young . . . if you are the wife of the youngest son, then all the other sisters-in-law can ask you to do things, leave aside the mother-in-law. Um. And I remember that my father also left her to go to Uganda when I think she . . . she had a daughter, and then another daughter who died at three weeks, because of smallpox, and then a son . . . and then another son was born, and then I think my father left for Uganda.

Throughout Jitendra's responses, this series of themes is maintained: the mother sacrifices for others, including for him. And this first step is followed by the second, the pacifying and minimizing of the father's position, and the neutralizing of his claims on the mother:

> ...where he was in Uganda and she was in India...he did
> say that 'I don't want to call my wife'. [Their] relationship,
> if I speculate, was one of duty rather than love...[My
> father] had the status of being a second-class citizen in one
> sense – but my grandmother used to like him a lot.

The father is even allowed a compensation prize.

Once the obsessional has set up this family complex, then all he
has to do is wait for the father to go away. The obsessional pretends
that he has no sexual claim on the mother, and waits for the father
to die. But the Oedipal relations are not going to go away, even if
the father does die. So in a sense the obsessional is condemned to
waiting forever, and one aspect of the state of the obsessional is
that he is not sure whether he is dead or alive. The obsessional, then,
is so busy escaping from the real demands and problems of sexual
love, that he becomes wrapped in a timeless web of knowledge and
doubt. The rituals that he spins out to traverse these gaps hold him
like a gossamer in a world where he cannot be sure that he is alive.
The pathways of his escape-route form a labyrinth, and escape from
these labyrinthine tunnels forms a common theme for the phantasy
of the obsessional. At the centre of a labyrinth is the threat of death:
the obsessional hopes that Ariadne's thread will save him from it;
but, unlike Theseus, he becomes trapped in its threads.

But Jitendra's father had already returned: 'We never felt a distance from him...all our needs were satisfied...whatever time he
gave'. The ambivalence is accompanied by a ritual repetition of the
phrase – 'you felt, not a lot of time with you...but always your
needs were satisfied'. The repeated phrases constitute formulae and
prayers: the obsessional finds it difficult to distinguish between himself and this series of verbal prayers, all of them functioning to maintain the perfection and ideal position of the mother, by avoiding
conflict with the father. These phrases which reverberate through
his life are carved onto him, like the inscriptions on the graves in
a churchyard. In many ways, the obsessional finds that he is made
of stone. Even given this, Jitendra it seems can still make a claim on
his mother: he tells first how he is like his father (he is a 'rover' and
'not a good husband'), and then tells that he likes to think that he
is like his father in the 'way we related to our wives'. The phrase suggests that the wives are common; Jitendra's calm contains a claim
on his father's wife.

My next set of queries began with a number of questions about the
woman that Jitendra was able to treat as 'another woman', standing in for his mother. This is a relation where Jitendra was able to
play out questions about his love for his mother. (This is an important

relationship, and I will return to it later.) I then asked him questions about his relation to his own family, and about his mother's relation within their family. After this, I asked about his mother's relation to his father 'in the household', and finally, in this section, about his own relation to his father.

About his mother's relation to his father, Jitendra is ambivalent: 'Nothing could happen in the house without him ... giving permission', but 'she ran the family actually'; 'she looked after the children's needs ... but my father made the big decisions'. His own ambivalence to his father also revolved around this question of a supposed satisfaction of 'needs'. Out of this ambivalence there arises a feeling of being forced to love: Jitendra talks in a determined way, praising his mother, and describing her encouraging the children to read – 'she made sure we all loved it'. There is not here an abandonment to an idyll of love, but he is describing what she did with 'all' of them, not just with him. Jitendra tries to separate out the differences between protection, wants and needs in his relations to servants and his parents: 'If we were in danger ... we would go to our servants, not our parents'; 'if you wanted something, you went to your mum, not to your dad'; and in relation to his father, 'all our needs were satisfied ... always your needs were satisfied ... I felt ... I knew'. I had asked him how much time he had spent with his father in the four years before his father's death: 'whatever time he gave' was part of his first reply; 'you felt, not a lot of time with you' was part of his second. From his father, Jitendra says, he could get what he fancied. He had only to say, 'I fancy a nice cake', and as long as the servants had started to prepare for a break, his father would let him have it. He remembers one of the wives of one of his father's brothers: 'I fancied one of my aunties ... she was a very beautiful woman'.

When talking about the African woman, Jitendra initially had said, 'I have no memory of her'. When questioned further he says, 'I have no imagination of her ... I certainly can't remember'. He ascribes to others the knowledge that he has of her: 'it was common knowledge ... that she used to look after me more like her child, and in fact I preferred her to mum'; 'I think', he adds. Her name is 'Kwezi'. Jitendra has now talked to his mother about this woman; his mother says that Kwezi 'took a special liking for Jitendra', that he 'just became fixated in her mind'. In reply to more questions from Jitendra, she said that Kwezi gave Jitendra another name; his mother used this name for him and she sometimes still calls him by it. Jitendra's mother is very direct about his relation to Kwezi: 'You, you were desperately loved by this woman'. His mother denies that Jitendra spent much time with Kwezi, and Jitendra pretends to accept that the history, as he had understood it, was a myth. This leads him to start remembering his relation with Kwezi: 'one thing I do remember is that I used to eat food out of her mouth'. His memory of his mother satisfying his brother's demand for love was of her putting morsels into his mouth. When asked what he remembers of Kwezi, he 'remembers' a black and white photograph. He had presented his memories of his father's father and his mother's mother in this way: he had seen photos of them. This photo is of a scene 'in bright sunlight; I can see it now'; Kwezi is on Jitendra's left, 'next to a cooking pot'; 'I was just next to her', he says. 'I think I certainly ate with her – she might have cleaned me, washed me, and did everything. I'm not sure whether I slept, actually, with her. I can't remember that'.

But Jitendra is remembering now a lot about this woman. 'Certainly I spent the whole day with her', he says, 'from morning to night'. So she gave him care and love; food and a bed perhaps. His brothers, he says, must have been craving for attention from his mother; he 'got it from her [Kwezi]'. So in these first fresh memories of Kwezi – irrespective of whether they are true – there is an opening up of the reality of love as Jitendra experienced it as a small boy of two or three. I asked him whether he could remember Kwezi's husband: 'I can't remember him. But other servants I can remember'. The father is absent *also* in the case of this 'other' mother. With both his real father and his 'other' father, it is not that they are really absent, rather it is that Jitendra has pushed them into the background.

The complex of the 'other woman' is particularly strong with the obsessional. As Jitendra says, in some respects he is being like 'any man'; difficulties enough are produced by this idea of 'several' partners in love, an idea that is more consonant with the usual sexual loves of men for women than it is with those of women for men. But with the obsessional the 'other woman' motif functions so as to produce a loss of any possibility of satisfaction with the woman that the obsessional is with. It is buttressed with other strategies that have the same aim. The obsessional has a remarkable structure functioning within the operation of his desire: any single trait in his partner – it can be the positioning of a hair, or the angle of a fingernail – the slightest aspect of the other person can suddenly become the cause of an instantaneous loss of desire. Only the obsessional has this catastrophic functioning at play within his desire. The obsessional faces a real dilemma – the woman that he wants is a substitute for the mother that he idealizes – and it becomes impossible for him to have her. If the mother can have no lack, no failing, no weakness, she is a woman without desire. This is why the obsessional moves from the woman that he is really relating to, to an adjoining woman who has all the desire that phantasy can give her. The obsessional cannot bear anything that introduces a wounding or lack in relation to women; the realization that real sexual love is bought dearly cannot be faced by the obsessional. Instead, he insists on facing only the prospect of a problem-free and blissful state. In reality, he will encounter only difficulties, and will become tormented and consumed with preoccupations and doubt.

The last set of questions that I put to Jitendra began with the scene in his father's bedroom where both he and his mother are on his father's bed. I then asked him about his father's absences, and about his relation to his mother after his father's death, and what she wanted at that time. Then I asked Jitendra a question about his relation to his brothers, before moving back to his relation with Kwezi. He had been talking about what his mother wanted from his father: 'I don't know ... I would love to ask her that'. He had introduced Kwezi in discussing his brothers: he was with Kwezi in the sun. 'I loved the sun', he says. These three things run together: love, sun and Kwezi. His brothers teased him because he was 'darker than the rest'; they gave him 'black' as a nickname. The photo with Kwezi is the only one he calls 'black and white'. It is this photo that he returns to when I ask him again about her. This time he calls it 'Black and white. Slightly tinged yellow', for the sun. The last time he had described this photograph, he had talked of his clothes. Now he describes hers: 'wearing a little scarf on her head'. And there is another boy now in the photo, an African boy: 'It is sunny – I have a sort of, not a happy face'. When he had described the photo of his grandfather, he had said: 'he wears a turban, and [has] an extremely grim face'. Jitendra's relation with Kwezi forms a series of threads that link with almost all of Jitendra's family complex. Towards the end of these sessions, Jitendra remembers that his grandmother used to like his father a lot: 'You could see that she was fond of him too'. Talking about Kwezi seems to have allowed him to talk about his father's loves.

Jitendra talks about the nature of marriage to 'an Asian woman'; he knows the problems about the 'blackness of skin' of the African woman he loved. Concerning his mother and father he says, 'You would need to put yourself under her and his skin'. There are a variety of themes at work here: there is a sexual reference here to the mother; a reference to the sun with Kwezi; a reference to feeding from their mouths; and a reference to – if not attacking the father – at least getting under his skin.

The last questions that I had asked Jitendra were about his father's feelings, about leaving his wife, and about whether or not his father

was supported by his mother, as a man. 'There would be a lot of negative things coming out', he said, 'if my mother was frank'. There
are a lot of negative things now coming out in Jitendra's sessions,
a relating of negative to positive things that he had poor access to
in the past. The 'negative' is itself a term that probably refers to the
photograph of Kwezi. During the questions he had twice talked
about 'images and memories flooding in'. At the end of the two
sessions, he said, 'It's become so much more real again, talking
about it. . . . It surprises me how much visual imagery I have of it,
that I was not aware of'. He adds, ' . . . and you know in many senses
this world has no continuity with the present world'. Giving access
to this lost and hidden world is what the analytical work is about.
After some years of analytical work, Jitendra's memories will not be
as they are now; and his love relations will be able to find some
bearings in his descriptions of the past. The 'talking about it' is what
produces the change. But this is a painful process, and what a
neurotic, says Lacan, 'bears least easily'.

Therapeutic possibilities

In order to assess the prospects for Jitendra, I need to describe in
more detail than I have already the nature of the analytical work
that he has embarked on. Psychoanalysis, according to Freud, is a
way of intervening in the pain of human relationships; this mode
of intervention, unlike the chemical, electrical, or even surgical interventions proposed by psychiatry, is made up entirely of one medium
– that of words. And this, as Freud many times puts it, is enigmatic
and puzzling: how it is that words can have a causal effect on pain,
how it is that they can bring about a shift in human suffering. There
are further puzzling developments. The signs that human beings use
to communicate, or to misunderstand each other and the world, or
to convey their suffering, are an even wider class of realities signalled
by Freud as lying at the heart of the exchange between the analyst
and the analysand. The question arises as to the relation between
this very large class of signs and the more restricted, although more
articulate, verbal representation of the world. The English tend to
assume that a 'pre-verbal' world exists, that it constitutes the experience of the little child, and that it underlies the functioning of words.
The Lacanian schools differ: they assume that any human experience
is determined by the already existing world of words that gives shape
to the relationships of the parents of the child. Symptoms are outcrops
of such underlying structures, the determinants of which pre-exist
the birth of the child; according to this view, feelings, phantasies and

drives are equally structured by these underlying determinants of language. This helps to explain why the interchange of words in analysis can have such a surprising effect, and also why it is words that Jitendra will have difficulty with. Symptoms are labile, they shift. The underlying structure they are expressing is, on the other hand, much more stable, and it is this underlying structure that is brought to light by the chains of free association produced in the analytical session. It takes several years for the detail of the structure to become apparent, but the beginnings of this process can be seen to be at play in Jitendra.

The contract that the analyst agrees to as much as the analysand is that one party will attempt to say everything, and the other listen – to what is barely being said, or merely alluded to between the lines of what is said. Very little in this set-up is self-evident. The associations that the analysand is asked for form chains that constitute a structure. Such a structure will have determined Jitendra in the main outline of his history, particularly in his love relations, up to this day. In order to perceive the links in this history, the analyst is asked to listen while subtracting every effect of his own ego – a commitment as difficult to fulfil as that of the analysand, where every association, no matter how seemingly insignificant, is part of the material demanded in the contract.

Three things are important. The first is that all that is asked for is a commitment to this (very peculiar) mode of speaking and listening. That each side of the contract is impossible to fulfil to the letter does not matter. A desire to work in this fashion is sufficient for results to emerge. The second is that the functioning of the ego gets in the way of this discourse – the ego structures object to the pursuing of the chains of free association. The aim of the free association method is to side-step the ego, to catch it off guard, and to gain access to the material that the ego would rather keep hidden. Surprise is therefore a very central function in the overcoming of the ego's resistance; the analysand tries to gain access to repressed material, and the analyst introduces effects of surprise. The overcoming of the resistance, in other words, is a task that the analyst, rather than the analysand, has to tackle. With the third factor things are different: the various theories that the analyst and the analysand have about the world are to be discounted, as representing distorted and misunderstood versions of the material that the work is seeking. So there needs to be a Socratic discourse at work, a logic of question and answer, where any of these theories is likely to be overthrown. The analysand needs to be able to tolerate the construction and the maintenance of this discourse. In this respect, Jitendra is already well advanced.

The course of therapy

The preliminary interview – prior to the sessions – already sets in motion some of these processes. Their continuation generates the succeeding three phases of analytical work: analysis has a beginning, a middle and an end. Many people do not continue as far as this end; those who do take a number of years to reach there, and the obsessional will take somewhat longer than the hysteric. For the obsessional to reach the end of an analysis takes perhaps seven or eight years. But there is no need to wait so long for changes – many of them considerable – to come into being. After three 'sessions' Jitendra can perceive many changes: the changes in his remembering of the memories of Kwezi are remarkable.

As to the form of the work, I will see Jitendra for anything between one and six sessions a week. The actual number of sessions will vary as the work proceeds, depending generally on a variety of factors: on how many sessions Jitendra is able to make, on my judgement of the intensity of the work, and on whether or not the compactness or the relative spread of the session across the week needs to be varied. For much of the work, it is likely that I would be seeing him for perhaps three sessions per week. If he were commuting for analysis, I would use a different scheme, generally seeing him for at least one session a day on the days when he is in London – perhaps two or three sessions a day, should the work demand it. I will see him for sessions of varying length, usually of about thirty minutes, but both longer than this and shorter than this. Ending a session in this way is an intervention into the work, as is an interpretation. Both function so as to break into the previous structures that governed Jitendra's view of himself and of his relations to others.

As Jitendra moves from his initial opinions – he 'does not remember' Kwezi – to the opinions that replace these, he starts to experience a brokenness in the structure of his opinions. The analytical work therefore generates a brokenness redolent with, and evocative of, the broken and unfinished love relations of childhood. So both the varying of the length of the session and the function of interpretation produce effects that initiate a transference – the bringing into the present of the broken love relationships of the past. The effect discovered by Kurt Lewin's student Zeigarnik in Berlin in the 1920s is that broken and unfinished tasks are remembered better than completed ones: these breaking effects of analysis therefore contribute to the remembering of the material produced in sessions. Jitendra's associations, and the effects on them of analytical questioning, are already showing such effects of remembering.

As for the development of the middle work, I will be trying to bring about a loss of ideals, and this will entail finding more real signifying terms from Jitendra's history, so as to produce a pathway that will both undo and replace these ideals. I will be looking for less 'should's' and 'have's' in Jitendra's discourse, for a diminution of the unpitying aspect of the super-ego. By means of this renewing of his history, I would also hope to be forcing on Jitendra a recognition of loss – the loss of his mother's love, and of any surrogate for it. One of the results of this will be the generation of an ability to focus on the problems of a love relationship without a flight being necessary into the trouble-free world of the 'other' woman; an ability also to tolerate the gaps that at the moment he vaguely perceives, and to actually put them to use in negotiating a relation of love.

Criteria for successful outcome

In the end, the work will focus on the 'fundamental' phantasy that will have been constructed out of the many day-dreams and reveries that Jitendra has produced. The power of this phantasy to set the stage for all of Jitendra's love relationships represents the power of what he cannot remember about the past, and brings about the impossibilities in his love relations in the present. The power of this phantasy needs to be broken, at the end. In a sense, in reaching such an end, Jitendra is able to make a conclusion; this was one of Lacan's favourite formulations. This is the point to end on; at the end of this analysis, Jitendra can conclude something about his desire.

Further reading

Benvenuto, B. and Kennedy, R. (1986). *The Works of Jacques Lacan: An Introduction*. London: Free Association Books.

Lacan, J. (1987). *The Seminar, Book 1: Freud's Papers on Technique, 1953–54*. Cambridge: Cambridge University Press.

Roudinesco, E. (1990). *Jacques Lacan and Co: A History of Psychoanalysis in France, 1925–1985*. London: Free Association Books.

Schneidermann, S. (ed.) (1993). *How Lacan's Ideas are Used in Clinical Practice*. New York: Aronson.

5

PERSONAL CONSTRUCT PSYCHOTHERAPY

The therapist

My background is that I completed training as a clinical psychologist in 1962 in the home territory of Hans Eysenck and behaviour therapy. I came across George Kelly's personal construct theory shortly after that and found, to my pleasure, that it was opposed to both psychoanalysis and behaviour theory.

I became more and more attracted to personal construct psychology (PCP) and found myself using its philosophy and psychology as well as its methods. My therapy work as a clinical psychologist in the Department of Psychiatry at a London medical school started 'slipping' more and more from behaviour therapy into the PCP framework. By 1980 I decided to leave the university and set up the Centre for Personal Construct Psychology in London. One of the centre's main sections has been the teaching of personal construct psychotherapy to diploma level, now recognized by the UK Council for Psychotherapy. So I have been involved in helping others become psychotherapists for several years; but like many others, I have had no formal training in the practice of psychotherapy myself. I am not counting here general workshops and short courses on counselling and psychotherapy skills.

There were four aspects of personal construct theory that attracted me away from behaviour therapy. I work with a philosophy that says that there are always alternative ways of construing (interpreting) events, and that no-one need be the victim of his or her biography – although we can become victims if we construe it that way. The therapist enters the relationship knowing they know nothing except how people may be helped to become more as they wish to be. The therapist's only job is to try as far as possible to enter the client's world and gain some understanding of how that person's construing of that world leads to the problems they are expressing. An essential ingredient in doing this is for the therapist to 'suspend' his or her own personal values. Only when these are out of the way can the therapist really listen and try to understand the world of the client in a 'true' sense. The theory gives no statements of how a person *should* be. All this makes personal construct psychotherapy useful in a trans-cultural context. The only values that matter are those of the client.

Another important aspect for me is that the person is seen as an entity – construing is about experiencing. There are no artificial distinctions such as between thinking and feeling. That does not mean that the client may not construe them as separate, which happens in particular in Western cultures where the norm is to think in terms of a body–mind dichotomy. Again it is the client's construing that matters in personal construct psychotherapy, but the therapist will be seeing the client as a whole being, as a form of motion.

Finally, the theory does not dictate the methods the therapist must use to help the client reconstrue. The therapist has a very complex theory to guide him or her (over four hundred pages in George Kelly's *The Psychology of Personal Constructs* (1955/1991)) about how we may go about the business of experiencing and making sense of the world, and it is pitched at a very high level of abstraction so that it has no specific content. We have created ourselves and can re-create ourselves by reconstruing our world. Within the embrace of this very explicit theory and philosophy, the psychotherapist can use any technique they choose *if they think it will help the client reconstrue that particular aspect of their personal construing world.*

George Kelly did, in fact, create three methods that the personal construct therapist may decide to use. These are the repertory grid, the self-characterization and fixed role therapy. In this instance, Jitu was asked to complete a self-characterization as part of the initial data collection process.

In conclusion, I would say that I now work exclusively within the confines of personal construct theory and its philosophy and do not feel the necessity to 'borrow' from any other approach.

Further information requested

At this stage of the sessions with Jitu, I see myself as collecting data. I would not normally have asked for such an extensive personal history as we have here. Much of personal construct therapy concerns itself with how persons are construing themselves and their lives at the present time. This may include much that the client thinks important that occurred in the past. If that is the case, as with Jitu, then the therapy will explore those concerns as long as they continue to dominate the picture. But there is nothing that says that exploring the past is essential. I quote the following from Kelly because it illustrates a number of important points and is relevant to Jitu's concerns:

> Historicalism is usually taken to mean that the course of events, once it is set in motion, elbows its way past the present and thrusts itself into the future . . . That is not for me.
>
> [As for] ahistoricalism, the phenomenal present is a pretty small sample to work from, much too small, I'm afraid. So ahistorical-ism, while emphasizing certain phenomenal points that stem from our postulate also, still tends to blot out parts of the record that we would have to consider important. Indeed, our model of man-the-scientist perhaps attributes a greater significance to the sweep of human history than does any other current psychological scheme.
>
> (Kelly 1959: 5–6)

This quotation mentions Kelly's model of the person as 'a scient-ist'. Kelly suggested we look at people 'as if' we are all doing what scientists do. That is, we erect a theory (a construct) about how things are; we make predictions on the basis of that theory; we then test out that theory and look to see whether or not our wager has produced a winner or whether we need to think again. The unique feature in this model is that behaviour becomes our personal way of putting our interpretations of the world to the test.

My questions to a client will usually be framed in such a way as to elicit some idea about what is being put to the test by certain behaviours. In my questions to Jitu, I only asked two that elaborate the already extensive personal history. For no particular reason, except to make the picture clearer, I asked how many children he had and he said he had two. The second question I thought more important: 'Who won over the religious issue with regard to bringing up the children?' I felt, on reading Jitu's history, that he may have some concern with the need for control over events. His reply was very helpful, and indicated that he lost:

> Ah, Well . . . yes. Winning and losing became, became the theme. There's no doubt about that. But it wasn't like that in the beginning.

Jitu then moves into the importance he attaches to his Indian culture:

It was in their [the children's] interests to have a positive
view and memory of what happened. OK, part of it is to do
with my sort of loss of my background, but that is not, you
know, that is not sufficient explanation. If I have a rich
memory of things, it would still have to – they would still
have to know about being Indian, and so on. Commensurate
with being of Irish parentage – half-Irish parentage. But also
taking into consideration the context of living in an Anglo-
Saxon society. So all these were relevant in my view, and in
a way they were exciting situations to discuss, to give
children good values, adaptive values and not values that
were false. But unfortunately, it became I think for my wife
a situation of fear, and she responded by pretending, as
though the issue didn't exist. She may have her agenda . . .

I note here that Jitu did not ask her what this might be:

I don't know, but I, as I saw it, my children were not getting
the acknowledgement, er . . . benefits of having an Indian
father.

My remaining questions were all about the present. The first, linked
to the above, was about how he saw his present relationship with
his wife. He replied that things have become polarized:

What were . . . differences, have now become polarities. And
that's very hurtful because . . . what I, the way I wanted to
resolve them, is to integrate them in some way. And if you
like it has moved further along the direction where I didn't
want to go. So there is the sad side and the side which I
accept.

My next question concerned giving two examples of situations
in which he experienced anger and rage and how he showed these
feelings. His first example was in early childhood with his brother:

We were I think sitting eating dinner. I forget the context of
this quarrel. And he sided with my younger brother, and I
was extremely angry – to the extent that I think I grabbed
him by the neck and held him down, although he was
stronger than me. So it was, if you like, anger, terrific anger
and rage, er, but it was, you were helpless, it couldn't
be . . . found vent.

He then cites an occasion when he saw a girlfriend going down the
road hand-in-hand with her ex-boyfriend. When he later confronted
her with this she 'seemed to fob me off. And I was quite angry with
her then. I was quite furious'. He showed this by just walking out of

the house. A third occasion was when a registrar at the hospital made a comment to him about people being ill and not being responsible, when Jitu had himself just been ill. Jitu says that he had, in fact, not informed the hospital that he would not be coming in. There was also some personal dislike of this registrar who 'was a very sadistic man'. He says:

> I couldn't take it, and when he made a negative remark, I remember my body shaking, but I didn't say anything [*pauses*] . . . I am learning to be more angry now. I occasionally feel rage but that rage is quite overwhelming for me. It devastates me. Um . . . I think rage is a very negative feeling . . . I think rage is, er, almost in my books by definition, er, destructive.

The next question was designed to gain more insight into how Jitu actually sees his problem. First, I asked how he would diagnose himself if he presented as a patient? He acknowledged that he gave a psychiatric diagnosis of himself, saying: 'If you look at a medical model of diagnosis'. I would normally have followed that up by asking in what other ways he might look at diagnosis, but I already had more than enough information. The second part of this question concerned what the referral might say. He again replied in a standard psychiatric way.

The next series of questions is part of a specific procedure used in personal construct work to elicit a person's views about aspects of themselves that they want to change or already see changing. In Jitu's case, it was about being a young man moving into young middle age. The questioning and Jitu's answers are as follows:

F.F.: What are the advantages of being a younger man?

Jitu: [*thinks*] . . . You have more energy. Physical energy. Your wistfulness for relative youth is a reflection of your having second chances at certain things. Er – either being, re-relating, er – either doing physical things like climbing mountains, which is one of the things I would have liked to do . . . But also in terms of the opposite gender, I think a chance to re-live certain relationships, constructively, rather than in stereotypical ways, which is what I have done probably, in early years . . .

F.F.: What are the disadvantages of being a middle-aged man?

Jitu: [*thinks*] . . . I think, er . . . loss of sexual attractiveness . . . pure sexual attractiveness on the street level. Er [*thinks*] loss of choice in where one could move . . .

F.F.: Are there any advantages of being a middle-aged man?

Jitu: [laughs] ... I think you don't have some of the anxieties and emotions which accompanies the anxieties of this younger man, you know, anxieties of identity. In middle age you have got some idea of who you are ...

F.F.: Are there any disadvantages in being a young man?

Jitu: Well, I would say the disadvantages of the younger man are the advantages of the middle-aged man, and vice versa.

After this series of questions, there was one about what he would need to happen in order to call the therapy a success. He replied:

I wouldn't use the word 'success' personally. Because that would not be an objective in the beginning. I think it is a process, and certainly it has already changed me as a person. On the conscious level I would be saying, 'Let me see what happens', although on the unconscious level I think I might be looking for answers. It would be a very constructive exercise – I don't know whether exercise is the right word. I would not want to categorize that – I think whatever the outcome, that's what you've got. It's like going to a funfair, going on the rides.

That same question was asked by other therapists in slightly different ways, but each provided some very helpful insights into how Jitu sees his future self. One point that came out was about change:

In many senses ... I ... this would have to be a final template. I am not saying that, that you stop growing [laughs], but I don't want to be a two-year-old now at seventy [laughs] ... I would like something much more, um, permanent now ... I can't keep changing. I feel the options to change too much are limited.

To a question about what information he would hope to get to enable him to bring therapy to a satisfactory conclusion, he replied:

... therapy would be just a means of accelerating you along the sort of direction you want to go anyway ... Not necessarily a destination in mind. I wouldn't bring issues to be resolved necessarily, but certainly my father's death would be an issue that I would have to come to terms with. Um ... the issue about middle-age or the issue about coming to terms with, um, disappointment and limitations, would, would have to have some sort of resolution for me, definitely. Um ... I would really like to know a little more about myself as a man in relation to a woman, rather than as a person or a human being. I have a very vague idea of me as a person, or as a human being. I am much clearer as a man, if you like. Um, because I was thinking about myself, and I always refer to myself as a man first, than to [say] as a human being or person. It's funny. It's my identity. Um . . . I would most like to be opened up there, but I think – I think all the other issues are related to that, as I see it.

Lastly, I asked Jitu to write a self-characterization, giving him the following standard instructions:

> I want you to write a character sketch of Jitu, just as if he were the principal character in a play. Write it as it might be written by a friend who knew him very intimately and very sympathetically, perhaps better than anyone ever really could know him. Be sure to write in the third person. That is, start out by saying: 'Jitu is . . .'

Michael Jacobs commented that, 'Jitu was given this task when we first met, but each time we met again he had not yet completed it. At our last session he gave me the final [last] version, with the accompanying description of it':

> You see, it is interesting. I did four self-descriptions. And they have been lying all over the house. Last Friday, my ex-wife rang me and said a relative had been taken ill, could I take over the children. So I didn't do much work. But I did it this afternoon. But what I am saying here, actually runs through all the things we've been saying. So in a way, I'm not sure, I don't think I'm very good at characterizing; but I have put words and thoughts as they have come to me. And it may seem disorganized. If you want me to write it out . . . I could do. It has been a fascinating exercise for me. I think I am going to continue doing it outside of this. Because it's certainly given me a tool to look at myself. And really it is, it is not an easy exercise. Um . . . I mean, I . . . I . . . it's fascinating. Anyway, I'll give you what I thought, what I wrote this afternoon. It doesn't say things like, you know, how I handle X situation or Y situation; or how I look, or how I relate. It's very much – soft. So I leave that . . . If you think it should be different I've got three other pages. If I find them, I'll give them to you as they are, because I have done them over time. They are on the back of envelopes and things like that.

What Jitu provided is this:

Scenario   *Here and now*

*A man   ⎫ situational and
   An Indian   ⎬ contextual   *definite*
   Human   ⎭ vague
*Shies away from 'PERSONALITY'. . .
   acknowledges DEPTH, UNCONSCIOUS and
   SPIRIT as realities
*A man searching for himself . . . for *GOD*
   Walking a TIGHTROPE – between
   Good/Bad (Evil) veers towards EVIL –
   GOOD is a STRUGGLE (STRUGGLING)

At a Watershed – bigger and better things
                       – looking into ABYSS of decay/death
                       – shaking off the PAST
                       – choosing the FUTURE

At the Edge   – cutting edge
                       – falling off the edge

   Easy to call myself Good, more difficult to
   admit badness (GUILT)

Awareness   – Selfish/self-centred . . . Self (Soul)
                       – Good/bad; light/dark; order/chaos
                       – Need for action – roles/expectation
                                              – tendencies
                                              – Evolution/Salvation
                                              _____

Easy-going, Comfortable, Pretentious
          refuses to collude/confronts
Need to be accepted . . . liked, loved
                       loved unconditionally

Ability to accept and take a lot (esp. –ve)
Needs to learn to accept +ve (Self & others)
Ability to *GIVE*
Understands others but only through himself rather than for
themselves
                                              _____

Alone/Isolated

Assessment

Having now had a glimpse of how Jitu sees his world, I need to formulate a 'transitive diagnosis', which means that:

> we are concerned with transitions in the client's life, that we are looking for bridges between the client's present and his future. Moreover, we expect to take an active part in helping the client select or build the bridges to be used and in helping him cross them safely. The client does not ordinarily sit cooped up in a nosological pigeonhole; he proceeds along his way. If the psychologist expects to help him, he must get up off his chair and start moving along with him.
>
> (Kelly 1955/1991, Vol. 2: 153)

My diagnosis has three aspects to it. First, it is couched in the language of personal construct theory and uses, in particular, the 'professional constructs' it provides. Second, it is largely my perception of the client's construing system both in terms of content and in terms of process. Third, it is essentially the planning stage of therapy. Without a diagnosis, a personal construct therapist cannot start therapy, and its formulation may need several sessions in order to collect enough data. Of course, as I believe in Jitu's case, reconstruing can be initiated by the data collection process itself. Lastly, the transitive diagnosis is expected to change as more information comes to light and as the client and I move forward. The underlying issue is that a therapist should not embark on any change strategy until he or she has some idea of what that strategy is asking the client to face.

I am therefore looking at the data available from the perspective that Jitu is a 'scientist' whose behaviour is the experiment he conducts to test out his views, interpretations (construing) of his world; as someone who can change by construing events differently; whose construing of events may not be adequately reflected in the words used; and in the full knowledge that I have to test out all my ideas at some point since I may well be wrong.

I look for areas of possible movement and also areas in which he seems trapped. There are four aspects of Jitu that I think should be looked at and which will no doubt turn out to be closely related:

1   There may be some pre-verbal issues that are causing problems for him. In personal construct terms, this is to do with construing at a low level of cognitive awareness; this is, similar to the notion of 'unconscious', but there are no 'dynamics' attached to it.
2a His apparent sense of a lack of identity. By this I mean that he has problems in construing himself; he is not clear of the core ways that enable him to say 'this is ME'.

2b Connected to this he may have a problem with role relationships in the personal construct sense; that is, he does not seem to be skilled at attempting 'to understand the understandings of others'.

3 In terms of his construing system, I will be looking to see whether his sub-systems of constructs are fragmented; that is, there seems to be no superordinate construing that holds them all together. It is here I think we may find the connections for which he is looking.

4 He has partially made himself a victim of his biography. In some sense he has made himself a prisoner of his past.

Vulnerability and pre-verbal issues

I note that in the self-characterization Jitu says nothing directly about emotions, although I am sure they are intimately bound up in what he does say. The point I note in his discussion of his anger, but of rage particularly, is his feeling of impotence. The rage seems to take over and to leave nothing. I equate these feelings with those of the powerless child. In the examples of rage he gives, it seems to occur when a particular role he has established for himself is shown not to work. I sense that he falls back on pre-verbal construing because of his ill-formulated sense of self. He says something along these lines at some point: 'It is, I would say, a tragedy for my own life, I think since the age of ten I have not really dealt with feelings. I have to act a certain role . . .'.

Another possible source of Jitu's feelings of anxiety and depression, is shown in his unusual self-characterization (which is unusual, but there are no right and wrong ways of doing things in personal construct therapy, so what Jitu has given me is all that matters). He says he is 'walking a tightrope' between good and evil and that he veers towards evil and that to be good is a struggle. I think this struggle may relate to being 'at the edge' and to the danger of 'falling off the edge'. If I look at what Jitu wrote in his terms of good and bad, it comes out something like this:

The tightrope
- searching for self/Soul/God *vs* selfish/self-centred
- good – a struggle *vs* evil – quite easy
- light/order *vs* dark/chaos/looking into an abyss of decay/death
- the future, bigger and better things *vs* falling off the edge

Being 'good' is a struggle, and perhaps all too often he finds himself behaving in an 'evil' way, which has very serious implications

and no doubt leads to feelings of loss of control and of chaos, decay
and death. The experiencing of such chaos I interpret as leading
to extreme anxiety as Kelly defines it: 'an awareness that the events
with which we are confronted are outside the range of conveni-
ence of our construct system'. I hypothesize that, when Jitu finds
himself at the 'bad' poles of his dichotomous constructs, he experiences not only considerable anxiety but also depression. For instance,
he says, 'there is a part of me that feels a sense of meaninglessness
at times, a sense of confusion, a lack of direction . . . a lack of flow
. . . a lack of connectedness'. All our construing is linked into a personal construct 'system', so it is no surprise to me to find here the
issue of 'being connected', although I prefer to link this to the issue
of identity.

'Vulnerability' comes up in a number of ways. First, in response
to Michael Jacobs' comment: 'I then observe that there is a protectiveness about him, which is very important to him, but keeps me
away'. Jitu replies:

> Yes, I think that's right . . . I think I would feel vulnerable [if
> the therapist were to be a 'bit more violent with him to get
> him to open up'] and I think for me to be vulnerable is a
> very hard state to be. I have had that experience. I think it's
> a difficult way of living and I am not sure how much I can
> cope with it, to be honest.

And later he says:

> My deeper interest in therapy and in my own work did arise
> at a time when I was very vulnerable . . . I felt vulnerable
> when my previous programme or attitudes or relationships
> weren't working and new problems came in.

We are likely to be vulnerable if the roles we have created to deal
with life are found wanting and we are thrown back on to our knowledge of our 'self'. If that sense of identity is not substantial enough
to sustain us, then there is likely to be an experience of something
approaching terror at the emptiness when some response as a person
is required.

The relationship between Jitu's sense of vulnerability and pre-
verbal construing is not clear to me, but I think it may well be
present and important. Jitu seems to think there is a need to explore
his relationship with his father. He is no doubt right, but I will not
pursue this until I get a clearer picture of what might be involved
here. What I am prepared to hypothesize is that, for some reason,
Jitu was not able to develop a strong sense of self as a young child.

A search for identity and connections

The theme of a search for identity occurs throughout what Jitu says about himself. For instance:

> I think what I would like to have an experience of now . . . is to get some idea of me as a little boy . . . I have very few memories of anything before the age of six or five.

It is argued that the only reason we can turn our reflections back on ourselves is because we have clear notions of who that self is. It is as if Jitu, a child in the middle of a large family, seems to have lived through the family and his place in the family, rather than developing a firm sense of his own identity separate from the family.

He also says that one advantage of middle age is that 'you have fewer anxieties about identity'. Towards the end of enumerating the advantages of middle age he again says: 'It's my identity – I would most like to be opened up there – I think all the other issues are related to that'. I agree with him. Jitu's search for his 'self' is also, I believe, directly related to his difficulty in understanding others: it is difficult to believe you are understood by others if you do not understand them or yourself.

There is a second strand in Jitu's self-characterization which is to do with knowing oneself and others. I find it difficult to identify the overarching construct, but it seems to be something like 'alone/ isolated/concern with self' *vs* 'self/Soul'. The implications attached to this go something like the following:

- concern with self/alone/isolated *vs* self (Soul)
- a man searching for himself *vs* a man who has some idea of who he is
- understanding others through himself *vs* understanding others for themselves
- needs to be accepted/loved unconditionally *vs* accepted by others *as a person*

I suspect it is to polarities such as these that he is referring when he says 'you can feel the tearing apart of the polarities in yourself at times'. One personal construct corollary I use here is that of 'fragmentation'. Fragmentation is not a problem in itself, but it can be when the sub-systems of constructs making up the fragments have no superordinate sense of self to hold them together. And it is this core, superordinate part of the self that I hypothesize is poorly elaborated.

A major formulation centres around the idea that we cannot know ourselves if we have difficulty seeing ourselves through the eyes of others. This also makes me think that Jitu at times feels extremely lonely.

Therapeutic possibilities

I feel very positively that Jitu and I have every chance of being able to work together in our search for alternatives to Jitu's current ways of dealing with his world. The personal construct psychotherapist never looks for solutions, because she sees every 'answer' immediately asking a new question. What we search for are ways of helping the client get out of the various dilemmas he has created for himself, which will enable him to 'get on the psychological move' in the directions he himself seeks.

One of my main reasons for feeling that we can work together is that I think Jitu already construes (sees life) from a position compatible with a personal construct perspective and that he will find the model of interest. Our relationship will largely depend on my ability to see the world through Jitu's eyes and, from all I have read, I think he will be open enough to let me have more of a glimpse.

Another positive prognostic sign for Jitu is his view of the past in relation to the present. He says:

> But deep down there is the other bit of 'what is the point of bringing these things out?' Although you know it somehow, that they do connect, they are relevant, the realization is not so intense that you need to follow it through. There is a sense of starting from here and now, if you like. You know: 'Today is the first day of your life'. I know that sounds trite but it's not. The past is relevant, but also realizing the limitations of its relevance. The future is connected to the past but . . . [*Jitu pauses*] . . . not so tightly that the past is to be explicitly clear, or reaches towards the future.

Any mention of contraindications is best left to the section on outcome, since I see none in relation to my being able to work with Jitu or his being willing to experiment with the approach.

The course of therapy

The initial agreement

First, I will explain my approach to Jitu in more detail. In particular, I will emphasize that I do not have any answers to his problem; he has the answers, as he is the expert on himself. He will also need to know that he will be expected to do most of the work. This applies even more to what is done between sessions than to within sessions. Some of the time in the sessions themselves, we will spend designing new ways of behaving that he can try out with certain people – perhaps understanding others – that he meets during the coming week. This implies, of course, that we agree to meet weekly. I will then answer any questions he wishes to put to me.

Next, I will discuss with him how many sessions might be useful in the first instance. I will suggest that Jitu commits himself to eight one-hour sessions. We then both spend time assessing how we feel about what he has been able to make of the work we have done. There are then three alternatives. One is that we agree that Jitu has learned enough about himself to feel that he can carry the process forward on his own. A second is that we agree he has moved some way along the route he has designed for himself, but he does not feel confident enough to go it alone at the moment. In that case, we might agree to meet fortnightly for a while, and then monthly, and so on. Or we may think that some progress has been made but that there are still some issues to be looked at more closely. In that case, we will probably be thinking in terms of another six or eight sessions. That is how our contract will continue to work. In general, I will be thinking in terms of having twelve to fourteen sessions with Jitu. He could well move faster than that.

Methods that may be used

My first concern will be to get evidence that either shows my initial diagnosis to be more or less on the right path or that I need to go back to the drawing board. To clarify this, I need to get more information about how Jitu sees things now.

I am going to ask Jitu to write me a series of self-characterizations during the course of the therapy, as he has shown that he finds the method of interest even though (or because) it is difficult. These will not only give us both information but will also form part of the goal of helping him construe himself more clearly. My initial one will be about 'Jitu now'. Later ones may be: 'Jitu as I expect him to be when this therapy is over', 'Jitu in relation to his father', and so forth.

I will also almost certainly ask Jitu to complete a repertory grid. Not only does this provide a structure for the initial stages of therapy, but for Jitu it may enable him to see how some of the fragmented areas of his life are connected. He may find some difficulty with the initial stages of the grid to do with construct elicitation. I think he finds it fairly easy to think at an abstract level about things but not so easy to see how these relate to everyday events. If this were to be the case, then I would use the method of 'pyramiding' to show the connections. For example, the construct might be 'easy going' versus 'refuses to collude/confronts'. The general questioning would be about 'what sort of person is an easy-going person?' 'What does that person do that makes you know he is that sort of person?' The same takes place with the opposite poles. The bipolarity of construing is an essential feature of personal construct theory and I believe Jitu may take to this aspect, as he also talks about 'polarities'.

The major focus of the therapy

Providing my transitive diagnosis turns out to be more or less on the right track, I imagine my major focus will be on helping Jitu put himself in the shoes of others and work out what they think of their world in general and of Jitu in particular. If he has spent most of his time looking at people from his own perspective rather than from theirs, he will not find this task easy.

For this reason, I may use the process of 'controlled elaboration', which is a way of helping someone work with small areas at a time. For instance, we might start with ourselves. What do I think is going through his head now about what is going on? Likewise, what does he think I am thinking about him? A lot will depend on the strength of our relationship at a particular point in therapy because it has to be construed by both of us as 'safe'. Alternatively, I might suggest he starts construing the constructions of strangers. Television characters can be used. Here the question becomes something like: 'What do you think that person is thinking about the other person?' 'Is there any other possible interpretation?'

Focusing on Kellyian role construing may (but need not) give rise to some spontaneous memories of Jitu's early family life. If so, the aim will be to put verbal labels on these early experiences so that they can be looked at from the perspective of the present. Sometimes these early constructions can be 'updated' and decisions made as to whether they are useful or not. Sometimes they can be 'time-bound' in such a way that it is acknowledged that a certain event happened and that it says certain things about the person concerned, but that the past is the past and it is now not useful to carry it around in the present.

I will certainly want to know more about the meaning of being vulnerable in Jitu's terms. What, for instance, is the opposite of that? There may well prove to be some 'good' aspects to being vulnerable that Jitu would like to hang on to, as well as some 'bad' aspects to his desired state of 'not being vulnerable'.

If it proves to be the case that some pre-verbal construing relates to Jitu's feelings of vulnerability and/or rage, and Jitu still feels the need to explore this, then other methods can be used. For instance, I find the use of dreams helpful here. These can be used in the Gestalt-type 'here-and-now' manner. All interpretations must come from the client. All the time the emphasis is on how the client construes, so there is no place for therapist-inspired interpretations, or the use of third-party interpretations such as symbolism. All the personal construct therapist can venture is such remarks as: 'It seems to me that you must be feeling . . .'.

Problem areas

The main difficulty I expect to have in helping Jitu to change will be his probable use of hostility, in the Kellyian sense. For instance, trying to see the world and ourselves as others see us is not always a rewarding experience. Movement away from the desired state of being loved unconditionally to being liked for certain aspects of himself, but also seeing the need to change other aspects of himself, and perhaps not being clear what those aspects might be, all this could lead him to extort evidence to prove that he is all right as he is and that change is not necessary. It is more than likely that his uncertainty about his identity leads him to seek control over events, so that he can ensure life remains predictable. But change usually means giving up one's control over those aspects of the self that are changing, for a period of time at least. This could lead to a hostile way of behaving to indicate that there is really nothing to fear – change is really a long way off, even if it happens at all.

Hostility leading to resistance to change is regarded as a positive act on the client's part. Jitu will always know himself better than I will and he will be right to resist if he thinks we are moving too fast into uncharted land.

Criteria for successful outcome

As has already been said, there are no specific goals for personal construct therapy. In this it is in line with Jitu's own reasoning. Success means that the client feels he or she can deal with their day-to-day life in a more predictable and controllable way. Providing we can control the hostility by not encouraging change at too great a pace, I do not see why Jitu should not meet that criterion. In line with that, I would want to see that Jitu has some better understanding of others 'for themselves' rather than 'through himself'. Otherwise, I can do no better than to quote Jitu's own words: 'Therapy would be just a means of accelerating you along the sort of direction you want to go anyway'. I would like to have some statement from Jitu that this is how he feels at the end of his therapy.

Summary

From the relative weight I give to the early sections of this chapter, it will be seen how heavily personal construct psychotherapy is weighted towards the beginning stages. The diagnostic stage is so important that several sessions are usually devoted to 'collecting the data' so that there is a reasonable chance that the therapist is on the right track. Since there are no prescribed methods to help the client change, it is quite difficult to say how the therapy procedure might go. It is largely up to the ingenuity of the client and the therapist. However, whatever course the therapy takes, it is guided at all times by the current diagnosis of the issue and by the tenets of personal construct theory and its philosophy.

Jitu is an unusual client for me because he is currently fully functioning in the world. I am more used to clients who have temporarily given up the unequal struggle to remain active in the world. Having said that, I see Jitu as embarking on psychotherapy rather than counselling. He wants to elaborate his construing of himself, his identity, and that is not an easy task for anyone.

The challenge for Jitu will be to help me understand the hidden meanings embedded in his culture that will be strange to me. I have the strong belief that he will be able to do that and that we will be able to move along together.

Further reading

Fransella, F. and Dalton, P. (1992). *Personal Construct Counselling in Action*. London: Sage.

Kelly, G.A. (1955/1991). *The Psychology of Personal Constructs*. London: Routledge.

Kelly, G.A. (1959). *The Function of Interpretation in Psychotherapy: 1. Interpretation as a Way of Life*. London: Centre for Personal Construct Psychology (in conjunction with Wollongong: Personal Construct Group).

Kelly, G.A. (1980). The psychology of optimal man. In A.W. Landfield and L.M. Leitner (eds), *Personal Construct Psychology: Psychotherapy and Personality*. Chichester: John Wiley.

6 JOSNA PANKHANIA

BLACK FEMINIST COUNSELLING

The therapist

I was born in East Africa of Indian parents, and lived there for the first twelve years of my life. I have lived in Britain for 27 years. I have worked as a school counsellor with Asian girls, a lecturer with counselling responsibilities, a residential worker in a hostel offering individual and group counselling, and as a counsellor for women. Currently, I am working at a women's health project. As a member of the British Association for Counselling I have been involved in setting up a sub-committee called RACE – Race Awareness in Counselling and Education. I am also a founder member of ABC – the Association of Black Counsellors.

My counselling approach can best be described as politicized counselling, in so far as I do not see counselling as something that happens between two people in a vacuum. I believe that all people are affected by social, economic and political forces, and as a counsellor I need to be conscious of such dynamics. My counselling practice therefore draws on my training in areas such as person-centred counselling, as well as on my research and writing about the history of oppression. Politicized counselling for me is being open to the client's immediate world (i.e. the self, family, friends, community) as well as the wider social forces (e.g. economic, political) that have impacted upon them.

When I was working as a counsellor for Asian girls, I was confronted by the fact that part of the distress that some of the girls were experiencing had to do with the institutions in which they found themselves. One example was the social services children's homes. The cultural alienation of the girls in these homes was profound. The

Asian girls' identity was not recognized, acknowledged or fostered by their carers. As a counsellor, I listened to their pain and I tried to help them to cope with their grief and loss.

Outside my counselling work, I aimed to set up a hostel that would meet the needs of Asian girls who are not able to live with their families any more. This project materialized because eventually a strong group of women who were committed to setting up such a hostel came together, and because it was possible to get funding for such projects in the early 1980s. For me, this is when the link between the personal and the political comes together in a most powerful way. I am not suggesting here that counsellors should try to change their clients' material world through political action. I am simply saying that it is useful for counsellors to be conscious of the impact of structural inequalities on the individual.

My commitment to the process which enables people to live happier lives is expressed through both political work and counselling practice. The political work takes many forms: working with groups of people campaigning against the British immigration laws in order to highlight the racist and sexist nature of this British institution, and researching and writing about the history of oppression. My counselling work includes participation in ongoing training which aims to increase my awareness of the emotional world, as well as myself going through counselling in relation to my own experiences of pain and hurt.

The integration of the personal and the political world for me is crucial, because I see much of counselling as offering support to individuals who find themselves in profoundly oppressive situations. As a counsellor, I see it as my responsibility to continue to learn about my own and other people's emotional world. I also see it as my duty to learn more about the forces of oppression and to challenge them whenever I can. In this way, my counselling work informs my political practice, which in turn informs my counselling.

I adapt the Rogerian person-centred model for my counselling practice. Much of my work has been with working-class black women. (Black people here refers to people who experience European racism and includes people of Asian and African descent.) In this context, I would say that I work with a black woman-centred approach. Such an approach accepts the individual and recognizes the class, race and gender dimensions of their world. My experiences of sexism and racism have led me to feel close not only to black and white women but also to black men and other groups of oppressed people. In this respect, it is important for me not to define myself as a feminist counsellor but as a black feminist counsellor.

Further information requested

The first six years of life

Jitu had said that he feels great rage and anger. To my question as to where he thinks these feelings are rooted, he said:

> I think they must be right from the beginning, where you are one of many children, and your needs are not satisfied . . . to the loss of, if you like, my abandonment – well the many abandonments in the family, plus the major one with my father. I think you could say that I am made of simmering anger. Only recently am I aware of that simmer . . .

Regarding the specific relationship between his parents during this period, Jitu said that he could not remember how his parents related to each other:

> No, I can't . . . I can see going to shopping with mum, but I can't see mum and dad together. Mum and dad used to sleep in the end room. His bed was on the left and hers was on the right. I can't see much interaction between them. No.

Jitu also talked about how he had a special relationship with Kwezi, the wife of the African servant, but that he could not remember details about this relationship. He said that 'she used to look after me more like her child; and in fact I preferred her to mum, I think . . . she used to feed me and everything'.

A painful incident that Jitu mentioned was when his mother hit him because he had soiled himself at his first day at school. Jitu did not talk about any particular hurtful experiences through play but talked about a woman who committed suicide in his neighbourhood. About this incident he said that 'it didn't register as though it happened to me'.

After the age of six

Jitu remembers the time when his father hit him when he was caught smoking and the times when his mother hit him with the rolling pin. During this period, Jitu did not see much of his father, because he was busy setting up his business. At the age of about ten, Jitu had a friend:

> We used to just spend time together. I fancied him at one time actually. I think I was in love with him, when we, I was about eleven. I loved his lips. But I – though it is very

far from feeling, looking back on it . . . and I think I wanted to kiss him at one time, but I never did.

Jitu also said that he still has contact with this friend: 'It's different now. I have not told him about some of my feelings'.

His father's death

To the question of how Jitu heard about the death of his father, he said:

> Oh gosh, I think nobody told us. But we were there . . . He wanted to die at home, so he was brought all the way from [a hospital in] Kampala . . . on Sunday morning we were all called to see him. And that was very upsetting. You were supposed to give him milk in his mouth . . . and then bid him farewell; and he was conscious, I remember. And I think, I think it is very hard to say that to your father. I think you did it mechanically, because mum said, 'do this' . . . I don't think we ever actually got in touch with our feelings at that moment . . . and later in the morning, we just had masses of people come to the house . . . Basically you children were out of the arena, do you know what I mean? I remember we were going in the garden which was quite large, and we had an old drum, a rusted drum, and I think three or four of us sat on it – it was a sunny day . . . and we didn't talk to each other much. I think we were all in our private feelings . . . If we did talk it was joking, almost like pretending nothing was happening . . . I remember going upstairs sometimes and so many people, all crying. My sister crying . . . and I think you didn't matter at that time, you know, as a person; because I mean, people were just going to . . . give their homage to him.

About the funeral Jitu has many vivid memories:

> And they made a bamboo stretcher. It's always made on the day, and they cover him with a white shroud; before that they probably clean the body, but none of the sons were asked – certainly I wasn't asked – and er, because I was too young or there were elder brothers – and I didn't go – only the men go to the funeral; but I didn't go with them. Er, nobody asked me, and even if they had I wouldn't want to go. It was my first experience of death. I didn't want to see dad's body personally. I want – I can remember how the shroud was taken. And I think they walked from there, from

my father's house to the cemetery, and, and, that's it. It was
Sunday, I remember . . . my eldest brother must have gone
because he has to light the bier. So he has to go, it's his
duty, and he did probably. Of course he did.

Jitu later said that he cannot remember any of his brothers crying
except when his eldest brother died suddenly about eight years ago:
'I saw my brother cry; And I couldn't take it. He upset me more than
anything else that was happening'.

After his father's funeral, Jitu remembers how daily routine took
over: 'I remember that evening, my mother would come and feed
the children'. With regards to the first week after the death of his
father, Jitu said that it was absolute routine:

You had to go to school on Monday. It was routine. You
were numb, I think, going back, and on automation – that
fact of father dying was feelingly touching you, but you
didn't express feelings. I remember just continuing with the
routines.

During the first year after the death of his father, Jitu said that he
could not remember his family members talking about his father.

Jitu also talked about how in the second and third year after the
death of his father, he coped with his grief privately:

Certainly in the first two or three years, there was a lot of
grief in me. And I can remember crying quite a lot at night,
going to bed. And I did say that you ascribed a sense of
personal responsibility to, for his death . . . And if anything
did happen to you, you would say that, 'Ah, because, you
know, you're fatherless. You are not an important person any
more'. You had this indirect . . . sense of not being important
as a boy . . . And it did affect you . . . any mishaps then were
probably feeding into this underlying sense of not being
worthy . . . the other major way that it affected you is the
way the material aspect of the life changed for us . . .

As a family, Jitu said that they did not cope with the death of his
father well:

I think we denied it to an extent. We didn't do it
constructively. I think it was one of these coping strategies,
which wasn't very well thought out. We could have done
those strategies but still acknowledged feelings.

To the question as to when Jitu found it was possible to think
about his father without feeling overwhelmed with grief, he said,

after thinking for a while, 'I don't think it ever is, actually. I don't think it's ever happened'.

Adolescence

Jitu talked about one of his happy experiences when he fell in love with a young Japanese woman: 'I think that's a wonderful time of my life . . . between the ages of fourteen and seventeen'. This relationship ended quite dramatically when the Japanese woman had to leave the country. After this, Jitu's woman friend did not write to him and he found this abrupt ending of the relationship difficult. Jitu also mentioned how the society in which he lived at that time was 'harsh . . . where interactions between young men and women were not permitted'.

Jitu's best friend during his adolescence was an Arabic boy whose father also died when he was much younger than Jitu. This friendship ended 'suddenly and inappropriately' just before Jitu left school. School, though, was a happy place for Jitu: 'At that time I was becoming a social being for the first time, in my own right, and I enjoyed it . . . I was popular at school . . . I did well at school'. Regarding life at home, Jitu said: 'I wasn't unhappy in my family. But I wouldn't say I was happy. I was not that happy'.

Relationships with Africa and African people

Jitu has many memories of life in Africa, and regarding the relationship between Indian and African people, Jitu said that 'It was clearly a negative relationship. There is no doubt about that. Because it was a relationship of the have's against the have-not's'. Jitu talked about the economic and social inequalities that existed between the Asian and African peoples. He also recalled how the British colonial system had instituted oppressive structures, such as the policy of unequal wages. Jitu went on to say:

> Oh yes. There were positive sides. I think, although the context was negative, definitely, the positive side was when people chose to ignore the differences they could relate at a human level . . . I would rather go to our servant if some boys were troubling us than to my father or my brother.

With regards to Indian people having African servants, Jitu said:

> Deep down I didn't like it. I think it is the wrong way to treat a human being. Even as a child I felt . . . it was terribly wrong. I think. If I am frank with myself it still upsets me

personally that I was part of that . . . and it also hurts me
that the whites were treated as special even by people like us.

Jitu was conscious of how some of his African fellow students struggled
to pay their fees and he did not have to. Jitu explained that:

Even when things were bad for us after my father died we
weren't still struggling to the extent that they were struggling
all the time. I think that has been a massive guilt complex
on me; I can feel that now talking about it here.

The transition from Africa to Britain

During the year before Jitu came to England, he experienced two
major losses: first, Jitu's relationship with his Japanese girlfriend
came to an end, and then when he was sixteen, his mother went to
England to join Jitu's older brother. At the age of seventeen, Jitu
took on a teaching job which he intended to do for a year until
he went to study law. However, half way through the teaching job,
which he was enjoying very much, Jitu was asked by his mother to
join her and her older son in England. All of this was rather abrupt
for Jitu. He was not happy about not being consulted. Jitu had no-
one to talk to about the move away from Africa. It is only as an
adult recently that he has begun to talk to his friends about the
emotions of this period.

Life in a new country

The answers to the questions about life in a new country are a
powerful description of the events. With regards to the question of
how Jitu felt about living in Britain when he first arrived, Jitu said:

Oh, I think it's a, it's – you feel dead . . . it was mechanical
living. Even until recently it was mechanical living . . . I had
an established place there. I had friends, I had community. I
was just reaching the age when the people knew me. I was
known, you know . . . You come here to London, and go into
this terraced property. You don't know anybody . . . I felt
dislocated.

Another significant aspect of moving to England was Jitu's loss
of the life he lived in Africa as a carefree young man. In England,
he suddenly had to shoulder new responsibilities. Jitu's mother in
her dislocation, for example, looked upon Jitu for financial and
other practical support, such as helping with the process of buying
a house, and so on.

Indeed, the move to England was a major change for the whole family. Jitu has many memories:

> My mother was working in a laundry doing ironing at six pounds a week. We had a large house in Uganda. We were [now] living in a single room. All four of us. With food in the drawers. I mean it was ridiculous. There was no bath. There was a kitchen with a bath which you put money in. It was all so new. You had this view of Great Britain, sort of advanced country, and you were living in this place, and you said, 'What is advanced about this?'

In London, in 'bed-sit land', Jitu did not have any friends. However, when they moved to Birmingham, Jitu made friends and 'they still remain friends to this day'. Jitu's experience of school wasn't positive either: 'You were a non-entity'. At medical school, Jitu's isolation did not get less. Jitu talked clearly about his experiences of racism from the other students and the Euro-centric curriculum that he had to follow. Nevertheless, Jitu was successful and he admitted, laughing loudly, that 'If you put me in a colony of baboons, I suppose I would adjust . . . or a colony of Gods!'

Marriage

Since the first interview, Jitu's relationship with his wife had deteriorated and they have separated. At the personal level, he feels much more comfortable about his separation for himself and for his children. At the interpersonal level, things have become worse: 'What were . . . differences, have now become polarities . . . So there is the sad side and the side which I accept'. The break-up of Jitu's marriage is yet another experience of abandonment and bereavement. Jitu said about the loss of his marriage that 'the grief was occurring over many years'. Bringing up the children seems to have been a major (though not the only) area of tension and conflict.

Jitu has two daughters, one of whom is thirteen and the other eight, and he loves them both dearly. The fact of being an Indian and a Hindu and married to an Irish Christian has raised many tensions. Jitu said that his wife certainly believed at the time when they lived together that 'the Bible was the only work of truth, literally so, and that any quotations about any other religions, or any experiences were invalid, by definition'.

Jitu's significant losses

'I think my mother's losses would be my losses . . . What they give you is their losses'. Jitu remembered the move in Africa from one town to another as a big loss. He also talked about moving houses three times in Entebbe, coming to this country, going to university, moving from Birmingham to London and then back to Birmingham, the break-up of his marriage, the loss of agility and stamina, the loss of his father and his brother.

To the question about how he feels about his losses now, Jitu said that:

> I think talking about them really, is, *really* is very
> constructive I find as a process. Just being – having
> somebody to put them together. Because . . . it is a very
> constructive process, and then somebody has given it to you.
> You have given it to them, if you like, or shared with them,
> and then you take it back with you; and then you work with
> it. And it can be quite . . . fantastic, I think.

Jitu's joys and sources of comfort

Jitu said that he enjoys being with his children, particularly the younger one: 'I have a lot of joy with her'. He also talked about the joy of nature, especially the trees, listening to music, 'being with a friend and being able to be completely at ease and talking – it can be a joyful experience'. He also referred to the joy of his first girlfriend, which Jitu feels can never be reproduced in his life.

Assessment

It has been a privilege to read Jitu's story and to get a small glimpse into his remarkable life. Despite the many experiences of loss and accompanying grief, Jitu has achieved so much and I rejoice in all of his achievements.

Jitu said that he has very few memories of his life before the age of six or five and that this period of his life he believes left a legacy behind. Jitu also said that his anger and rage are rooted in early child-hood experiences, when he was one of many children and he felt that his needs were not satisfied, as well as in the many experiences of abandonment in the family.

I am conscious that I may be treading on precious ground when I write about Jitu's relationship with his parents. Whatever I have to say about these significant relations I say with care and respect. My understanding about childhood is that we have all been hurt as children simply because of the unequal relations that exist between adults and young people. Some of us have been hurt more than others, and when this hurt impinges upon our adult life, it is useful to articulate, experience and re-evaluate every facet of the original hurt within a process of careful therapeutic disclosure. Thus, within the context of therapy, I might encourage Jitu to explore his childhood relationships with his parents. The wife of one of the servants also cared for Jitu when he was little, and so I might encourage Jitu to examine this relationship too.

The death of his father has had a profound impact on Jitu. Underneath the 'simmering anger' there is tremendous grief. I find it difficult to write about how painful this grief may be for Jitu. His father died more than thirty years ago and yet he has never been able to think about his father without feeling overwhelmed with grief. However, despite the grief, Jitu managed to do well at school. He was popular, made many friends and was successful academically. Within his family he was neither unhappy nor happy.

During adolescence, Jitu's experiences of loss continued when his first love, the Japanese woman, left and when his relationship with his best friend, the Arab boy, ended. Shortly after this, his mother left him to go to Britain, another distant country. A year later, at the age of seventeen, Jitu found himself giving up his newly found freedom to go to London to join his mother and brother. The transition from Africa to England was traumatic. Life in the new country was not easy for the whole family, and yet in many ways Jitu managed to adjust to the alienating environment well.

Jitu has great clarity of the wider socio-economic dynamics of his life both in Britain and in Africa. He is conscious of the dynamics of Asian people's experiences of oppression in Britain. This links to his awareness of the impact of the political economy on groups of people in the part of Africa he grew up in. Jitu is conscious, for example, of the impact of European colonialism and racism in Uganda as well as the contradictions that existed between the Indian middle classes and the African people. However, beyond the intellectual understanding, Jitu continues to carry guilt with him from some of the African experiences. I wonder what the impact of Jitu's experiences of racism in this country has been.

In some ways, Jitu's marriage has been another source of grief, and recently he separated from his wife: 'The grief was occurring over many years . . .'.

The middle stage of his life is also causing Jitu some anxiety. He says that it is a transitional phase for his development, and all the other issues that he has mentioned are 'in danger of it'. Two central issues related to this anxiety are related to coming to terms with the whole of himself as well as coming to terms with death. With regards to the question of death, Jitu had this to say:

I'm frightened of death. I'll be honest with you. I wish I could embrace death like I could embrace life, but you can't. I'm scared of death. Death means so many frightening things for me. In a way I would like just to melt inside it, if I could integrate things. I would like to be able to accept it.

Jitu also said he does not know why, but he thinks of death 'virtually every day'.

His search for meaning and the ethical dimension of life is very important to him. This quest for meaning includes a search for 'what is right or good behaviour, with good thinking or right thinking, with dharma and with not harming . . .'. The present is problematic for Jitu and he says that a part of him feels a sense of meaninglessness at times, a certain sense of confusion, a lack of direction, a lack of flow, and a lack of connectedness.

Essentially, my reaction to Jitu is one of wonder, great respect and sadness. Jitu is a loving, creative and an intelligent man. His many losses and grief have touched me deeply. If I was working with Jitu as a counsellor I would hope to help him to mourn; and once he has gone through this difficult journey, I would hope that he would be able to think of his father, his eldest brother, his wife and his other losses without feeling overwhelmed. I would also hope that he would be able to feel happy and joyful again.

Therapeutic possibilities

Amazingly, in many ways, Jitu's story is also my story. I am Indian, I grew up in Africa, my brother died when I was nine, I came to this country with my family and have experienced many losses, including the death of my father and then the death of my sister. All of this in some ways might be positive. I think that I would be able to offer Jitu genuine empathy and understanding of some of his experiences. However, Jitu's and my common experiences could also be negative if I were to over-identify with Jitu.

One thing that I do know that I would find difficult is Jitu's fear of death. There are for me also many unresolved issues with regards to the subject of dying. I am, for example, also frightened of death as a result of the deaths of my loved ones. I think that I would need to be very careful and self-critical when exploring the issue of death with Jitu. If I found that I was not really helping him adequately, I would aim to seek support from my supervisor in order to do so. I would hope that being rigorous about monitoring the progress in this area and seeking support when necessary might be positive.

The course of therapy

I start my counselling usually by having a discussion with the 'client' about the counselling process itself. In this session I try to find out what ideas the client has about counselling. I also explain to the client how I work, what my understanding of the counselling process is, in what ways I think that counselling might help individuals, and so on. The aim of this discussion is to find out if the client and I have similar aims and objectives regarding counselling or not. A lot of the women that I have worked with have no idea about the theoretical process of counselling, for therapy is not part of their culture. Most people, however, do know intuitively that talking to a person who is not going to think badly about them is comforting. And so, with this as a starting point, I explore with the client the finer details of this process, such as uninterrupted space, respect, acceptance, trust, personal responsibility and boundaries. I also talk about my own support and supervision structure and seek permission to discuss the case anonymously with my supervisor. Generally, by the end of this session, we arrive at a loose contract, which is clarified in more depth during the next session.

The second session usually lasts about two hours and I take down a written case history. This I do by allowing the client to talk about important relationships and significant experiences from their first memories to the present day. The client and I then discuss the areas that they would like to explore within the counselling relationship. At the end of the second session, a more detailed contract is usually formulated. This contract might include tentative areas that may be explored during counselling, details about the extent of support that I will offer and an agreement about boundaries. At this stage, there might also be a discussion about the possible difficulties that may arise for the client when exploring painful experiences from the past. The client's own support structures might also be explored. Finally, I would make explicit my commitment to the client to find their own inner strength and peace.

First six years of life

Jitu might want to start the counselling process by exploring his early childhood relationship with his significant others: his parents, his sisters and brothers, his aunts, uncles, cousins and other relatives, and his family friends. Jitu feels that the early years of his life have left a significant legacy. With regards to this legacy, it is important for me to say that I would not attempt to induce some form of hypnotic state for Jitu to explore his early childhood experiences. What I might do is to wait until Jitu felt safe and ready to remember the legacy. When the time was right for Jitu, I would do my best to ensure that he had adequate support to deal with the trauma of the recollection of the experience.

Jitu talked about many hurtful experiences from his childhood and I might encourage him to explore these further in terms of the emotional impact of these experiences. Regarding his relationship with the boy that he 'fancied', I would try to communicate to Jitu that I respect gay and lesbian relationships and allow him to explore his own sexuality if he so wished.

Father's death

Jitu's acknowledgement that he has never been able to think about his father without feeling overwhelmed with grief is most significant. I would want to encourage Jitu to mourn the death of his father in its entirety. I remember studying the different stages of bereavement in my counselling training, but until I went through that process of bereavement myself, I had little idea of the intensity of grief.

In many ways, Jitu's description of the day when his father died is similar to the day when my father died, and so within the counselling situation I would have to work very hard to ensure that I did not become engulfed in my own grief, that the space was Jitu's and not mine. I would want to give him a lot of time just to be with the feelings that were related to that terrible day when his father left him, never to return, how hard it was for him to bid his father farewell, and how alone he felt, because as a child he felt that he did not matter.

With regards to the final rites, I might want to give Jitu time to think and feel about the funeral and to be with all the emotions which that event created in him – emotions that he has carried with him, emotions that he may not have had the opportunity to explore since. I might also try to encourage Jitu to think about why he did not want to go to the funeral. Earlier on that day, he could not say goodbye to his father during the farewell ceremony. I imagine that all of this might have been an overwhelming experience. Jitu's mother was overcome by her own grief; his relatives in their sadness performed their duties. It seems nobody took his hand to lead him through the events that were confronting him as a child. Nobody held Jitu when I guess he could hardly stand up. Later, like many bereaved children, he felt in some ways responsible for his father's death and also felt very negative about himself. He had an 'underlying sense of not being worthy'.

Crying is difficult for Jitu, and so I might try to explore this issue with him. I believe that sometimes it is helpful to express our deepest cry. I would hope that I would be able to help him to weep if he wanted to.

The process of coming to terms with the death of his father might involve expressing the pain and anger of many years, by remembering both the good and the sad times. I might encourage Jitu to look at his family photographs to visit these times. If he felt comfortable with the idea, I might encourage him to talk to the people in the photographs, thereby rounding off unfinished business from the past in a small way.

When it felt appropriate, I might suggest to Jitu that he have his very own ceremony to bid his father farewell, and if he felt that it would be useful for him for me to be there, then I would be – indeed, I would be honoured.

Adolescence

Jitu was deeply hurt when his first girlfriend left him. Within the counselling context, I might try to encourage him to talk about the good times he had with this friend and to mourn the loss of this love. Gradually, I might encourage him to focus on the emotional impact of the break-up of that relationship. Finally, he might want to say goodbye to his first love. Related to all of this is the restrictive society in which Jitu grew up. He may want to explore if there are any ongoing issues related to having grown up in such a controlling society.

Jitu said that during his adolescence he was not happy in his family. I would see it as my role to support Jitu in his exploration of his unhappiness. Is there any unfinished business that Jitu is carrying with him from this period in his life?

Relationship with Africa and African people

I believe that the environment in which we live has a profound impact on us, both joyful and depressive. Contextualizing our own experiences within the wider social framework is sometimes useful in stopping us from internalizing the oppressive dynamics of society. Jitu is very aware of the impact of colonialism in Africa, particularly in relation to the oppression of African people. He is also aware of the many contradictions that existed between African and Asian middle-class people in Uganda when he was living there. Indeed, he said that he feels that it left him with a 'massive guilt complex'. Within the counselling situation, Jitu might want to explore this further.

The transition from Africa to Britain

In the counselling relationship with Jitu, I would see it as my role to offer him the opportunity to continue to express his thoughts and feelings from this period of his life. The move from Africa to England was indeed a major upheaval for him, and since he did not have opportunities to talk about his feelings in relation to this big change in his life at the time, there is a possibility that Jitu is still carrying today the distress from this earlier period in his life. Perhaps he needs to grieve the life he lost when he came to England. The process of expressing past grief might release energy that could help with the healing process and the resolution of feelings of powerlessness and isolation.

Jitu said that the experience of living in England was initially one where he felt dead. Within the counselling situation, he might want to make contact with the emotions behind the experience of feeling dead, not knowing anybody, mechanical living, and the experience of feeling dislocated.

Reading his responses to my questions about his transition to England and life in the new country touches me deeply; it is in many ways the story of hundreds of Indian people (myself included) who came to England in search of a better life. I felt it a tremendous privilege to get a small glimpse into Jitu's sensitivity and awareness about his new environment and his ability to adjust to an alienating society. Nevertheless, I wonder what personal price Jitu had to pay for this coping? Jitu might want to explore this area further.

Marriage

Jitu might want to mourn his marriage and all that went with it. Within the counselling context, he might also want to explore how he might like to continue his relationship with his daughters and his ex-wife.

Jitu has been and continues to be troubled by the great cultural conflict that he experienced in his marriage. The question for him is, what should he tell his children about how they should view the world? Their father is an Indian Hindu and their mother is an Irish Protestant. For Jitu, there is much 'conflict and suffering' associated with this question. Jitu is able to link his alienation within his marriage to the alienation that he experiences in the wider society. In relation to both forms of alienation, he talks about not being valued and not being recognized. He is conscious also of adapting to all these pressures rather than 'working through the process of adapting'. Within the counselling context, Jitu might want to work through this process by focusing on the price that he has had to pay in order to adapt. I might also encourage him to express the emotions that were put to one side as he adapted to hurtful situations. Perhaps the releasing of these locked emotions may set free energy for him to deal with the ongoing difficulties of his former marriage.

Problem areas

Jitu acknowledged that it would be easy for him to talk and intellectualize about his past experiences. While talking and intellectualizing is a useful exercise, it is not enough for the purpose of dealing with overwhelming grief. I might therefore encourage Jitu to make contact with the emotions of his experiences.

When I am working with someone who is rather cerebral, it is sometimes difficult to encourage that person to focus on the emotions and to express these emotions. One way to enable a person to express them is to encourage that person to focus on the physical blocks that are suppressing the emotions. These physical blocks might take numerous forms, such as a tense neck, backache, 'knots in the stomach', etc. Sometimes, the physical blocks are rationalized intellectually, and in such cases it might be necessary to explore this further. In so doing, the client may talk about how they believe that it is silly to cry; or they may be concerned about what the people next door might think, and so on. Such concerns need to be dealt with; then the process of removing the blocks can begin. At this point, I see my role as counsellor as encouraging the client to work towards removing their own blocks.

I do not know how difficult all of this might be for Jitu. My guess is that it might be very difficult and so I would want to be guided by him. I think that if he felt safe and supported, he might want to express some of the emotions that he has carried with him for many years. The energy that was used to suppress these emotions might then be used to deal with his feelings of abandonment. Hopefully, through this process, some of his past experiences might be integrated positively into the present.

For Jitu, the question of mortality raises many issues and he is frightened of death. I too am frightened of death. Thus there could be a problem in my counselling him. How can someone who has not come to terms with death help another person to accept death? I really do not know if I could help Jitu in this important area or not. I would hope that my own experiences might enable me to offer Jitu a deeper understanding and empathy. But is this enough? I do not know. My work with women has taught me that although we may share much common hurt, in the last analysis we all have to find our own road for our own journey. I would like to think that I might make a loving companion for Jitu on his journey even though I have my own journey to make.

Criteria for successful outcome

At the end of my counselling with Jitu, I would hope that Jitu is able to think about his father, his brother that died, his wife and his other losses without feeling overwhelmed. Finally, I would hope to see Jitu being less frightened of death and thinking of life with more hope, inspiration and joy.

Summary

The time has come for me to say 'Thank you' to Jitu. I have gained so very much through reading, writing and thinking about him. I feel very sad indeed that I shall never meet him. I wish Jitu goodbye and all the best in life.

Further reading

There are people who have written about politics and therapy or counselling, such as the feminist therapists (e.g. Baker Miller, J., 1978, *Toward a New Psychology of Women*. Harmondsworth: Penguin) or Andrew Samuels (1993) in *The Political Psyche* (London: Routledge). See also Tudor, L.E. and Tudor, K. (1994) 'The personal and the political: Power, authority and influence in psychotherapy', in P. Clarkson and M. Pokorny (eds), *The Handbook of Psychotherapy*, pp. 384–402, London: Routledge. To a great extent my particular counselling approach that I call politicized counselling, as described in my comments in this chapter, has evolved out of my work as a counsellor and as a community worker, and out of my research and writing about the history of oppression (Pankhania, J., 1994, *Liberating the National History Curriculum*. London: Falmer Press).

Acknowledgements

I am grateful for the support I received from a number of people while writing this chapter: my husband John Macdonald; my mother Maniben Pankhania; my friend John Sherry and the editor. Finally, I would like to thank Jitu for sharing so much with me.

7

CHRISTOPHER PERRY

ANALYTICAL PSYCHOLOGY

The therapist

I first read Carl Jung's autobiography, *Memories, Dreams and Reflections* (1963), when I was in my late teens and in a state of crisis. The book made a profound impression on me, not least because it contrasted so strongly with what I had read previously of Freud. But more importantly it influenced the whole course of my professional life.

My basic training in psychiatric social work at Edinburgh included an extended placement in the Jewish community in Manchester. These two experiences alerted me to the importance and difficulties of working with 'difference'. The training itself was based on the principles of psychodynamic individual casework and groupwork. These were grounded at that time in classical psychoanalytic theory, which felt incomplete to me. My first job was split between a psychotherapeutic community, staffed largely by Kleinian therapists, and an approved school, where my colleagues on the psychiatric team were a social psychiatrist and a psychoanalyst. These two settings provided consolidation and extension of what I had learned; and this was complemented by my both entering and training in group analysis as expounded by S.H. Foulkes, and amplified by the Jungian analyst Robert Hobson.

A loathsome degree in experimental psychology (it included only four lectures on Freud and two on Jung!) preceded a lengthy sojourn in India, during which I resolved to train as a Jungian analyst. On returning to this country, I obtained a post in a large NHS psychotherapy unit, where I worked primarily with adults, both individually and in groups, and I was supervised by analysts of classical Freudian, Kleinian and Independent persuasions. During my ten years in that post, I entered Jungian analysis and completed Jungian analytic training with the Society of Analytical Psychology, known in Jungian circles as the 'London' group. This has gained particular recognition because of its attempts, pioneered by Michael Fordham, to redress Jung's failure to address infantile and early development.

While strongly thinking of myself as a classical Jungian, I am indebted to psychoanalysis for its theoretical constructs and its rigorous application of clinical concepts, and in particular to the work of Donald Winnicott, in both its theoretical and clinical dimensions.

My approach to therapy is based on the mutually transformative influence that client and therapist have on one another within a strong but flexible therapeutic container, which consists of the setting, my reliable availability, the client's commitment and the practical arrangements, and, when necessary (and with the client's permission), my contact with significant others in the client's network. Within this setting, I seek to understand the client's suffering in terms of its causes and purposes, with the goals of increasing the client's conscious choice, facilitating development in their inner and outer worlds, and encouraging innate healing processes through the integration of previously disowned aspects of themselves (or 'sub-personalities', as I prefer to term them). Much of this work takes place through our joint attempts to notice and understand the ways in which the space between us is filled by projections from both parties, which distort the way we perceive, feel about and relate to one another. This is what is meant by working with the transference/counter-transference dynamics.

Further information requested

On receiving a self-referral, it is my practice to advise the client over the telephone that for the purposes of mutual assessment we may need a maximum of three ninety-minute sessions. And furthermore, that I might at the end of that time refer the client to a therapist or agency that I consider might meet their therapeutic needs more appropriately. My purposes in this are to emphasize the importance of the assessment process, to give me adequate time to think about the client's needs and to inhibit attachment, particularly neurotic attachment from my end.

In my opinion, Jitu lends himself admirably to this practice for several reasons. He is a consultant psychiatrist, unused to being in the 'patient's' chair, suspicious of his own craft and habituated to the role of 'observer'. One of my primary tasks in the assessment process is to make deep, meaningful contact with the client. And I judge the attainment of this goal in terms of being able to shift one or more of the client's major defences so as to release powerful feeling(s), a release which teaches me about the client's motivation, capacity to trust, curiosity and ego strength.

In the transcript of the first interview, there is a striking lack of reported affect and a tendency for Jitu to depersonalize himself (e.g. he tends to say 'one' instead of 'I'). As his story unfolded, I noticed in myself the gradual gathering of a congregation of feelings about which I was very curious and from which he seemed partly disconnected. These were: a tension between becoming himself and looking after others; the loss of his wife and children; the sadness resulting from an obliteration of early childhood and the loss of his inner child; the claustrophobia of being in the midst of a large extended family; the grief, rage, guilt and helplessness over his father's death; the feeling of being uprooted and transplanted at the age of eighteen into a foreign milieu; the subsequent feelings of alienation, dispossession and urgency to belong (as expressed partly by his marriage); the impoverished sense of self-esteem; the feeling of fragmentation – parts of the self scattered over India, Uganda and Britain; the denied thrill and the deadening dread of being at the watershed of mid-life; the fear of death; the possible guilt over surviving Jitu's brother's death; the complexity of feelings surrounding women and the feminine within himself. As I begin to grapple with these feelings, I start simultaneously to ponder on the defences Jitu had developed to cope with them, and I wonder how I would have coped.

Jitu is someone I might arrange to meet again. There are several areas of his personality and life which I wish to explore further, mainly because I need to know if he is willing and able, within a therapeutic milieu, to catch a glimpse of, beckon and befriend these many sub-personalities dissociated from himself (which he has put me in touch with) at the cost of perseverating the deprivations of his childhood and of the impoverishment of his personality. I will now outline some of these areas.

C.P.: Why is Jitu seeking the possibility of therapy *now*?

Jitu: Yes, tentatively, yes. Not definitely. Because there is a continual sort of awareness and pre-occupation with certain unresolved *things* . . . I'm not sure whether *it* is a problem or not. But something is bothering me . . . At times *things* have been desperate, yes, now is a *range* of time . . . [my italics throughout].

Here we can notice a feeling that oscillates between a specific feeling and a spectrum of feelings that seems boundless in time. Is there a connection? I pursue this line of enquiry and Jitu alights on the theme of *change*. By so doing, he demonstrates a capacity for self-reflection and talks about 'moving house, moving jobs, um, say a new member of the family, when my children were born . . .'. There is no further mention at this stage of earlier major changes, suggesting that these are too painful to recollect in an emotional sense. However, in his next sentence there is an allusion to 'disappointment . . . where *you* [my italics] feel you should be able to overcome that disappointment, where it is exaggerated, then you feel something more is happening to you than simply, um, a setback'. Thus far we have a watered-down reaction to change and a similarly diluted feeling of disappointment. I can understand these feelings in relation to the loss of the father; but I already have a suspicion from the first interview that Jitu's dominant function is that of thinking. I therefore feel bound to try to contact his feeling. I need to know more about his hidden feelings.

C.P.: Can you reflect more on the violent feelings within you? To what or whom are they directed? How can you understand and harness the energy contained within them?

Jitu: So it was, if you like, anger, terrific anger and rage, er, but it was, you were helpless, it couldn't be . . . found vent . . . I was furious . . . I was extremely angry . . . It was my fault . . . I remember my body shaking, but I didn't say anything . . . I occasionally feel rage but that rage is quite overwhelming for me. It devastates me. Um . . . I think rage is a very negative feeling.

Note the intensity of the feelings. And again:

C.P.: Is meaninglessness a living form of death for you?

Jitu: Yes, I would say. I think I would find meaninglessness suffocating. The word 'meaninglessness' as I saw in my own, say, marriage – that's the word that actually crossed my mind. Many times. This interaction is meaningless. That I would find very suffocating . . . And if you took it to its extreme, it would kill me. And I think I would actually physically die. In that situation.

C.P.: If so, how do you think it could be transformed?

Jitu: I think that there is meaninglessness in life – there's no doubt about that. It could be there; it is there. It is linked up with the loneliness part of me . . . I think that I believe that through your children there is the possibility of redemption. I believe that. [*Here is a sign of hope.*] Every relationship is an unlimited ladder of emancipation. [*'From whom?', I might ask.*]

> *C.P.:* When you lapse into silence during the interview, what
> is going on within you?
>
> *Jitu:* When I am silent, I am thinking whether I can say
> what is there – things bubble up, but it is not always
> possible to speak them to you . . . I would dearly like to
> tell you, but sometimes I can only say it to myself.

I go on to interpret this as shame, one of the most powerful and crippling feelings we experience, and one of the most hard to acknowledge. And, finally, Jitu is able to see that his depression may have a purpose, however elusive at present.

Another major area of enquiry is Jitu's relationship with the feminine within himself and without. The initial interview suggests to me a cool relationship between Jitu and his mother, for which the relationship with the African woman may have been compensatory. Jitu shares much information about his mother, but he also says:

> I remember her caring for me really, in all respects. Mind
> you she didn't – she was mainly physical care. Er . . .
> emotional care, perhaps one did get it – I, I did, I can't
> remember not getting it, if you like, I can remember her
> washing me, doing things, etc.

Later, I ask: 'Do you feel your attitude to the feminine and your relationship with your wife have anything to do with your relationships with your mother and sisters?' Jitu answers in the affirmative, but goes on to say:

> I had a tremendous longing for the feminine in my
> relationship, in my – it's difficult to put words to, but I
> have always felt the lack in my life of a feminine guiding
> principle . . . a terrific lack . . . of the feminine wisdom.
> Because my idea of the feminine wisdom arising is essentially
> Indian – it is an Indian woman . . .

His reply tends to confirm the hypothesis that Jitu was not close to his mother, and that this lack has contributed to him losing touch with the inner child, who does not exist before the age of ten, and who is lost in a large family.

Further information gleaned in the second interview included an elaboration of Jitu's mid-life crisis and his efforts to individuate; his relationship with death; the traumatic loss of his father and his fatherland; his motivations for becoming a psychiatrist, which included his father's death, his brother's career in medicine, and a throwaway comment about paralysis in one leg when Jitu was very young; and his goals for therapy, which include coming to terms with his father's death, coming to terms with disappointment and limitations in mid-life, knowing more about himself in relation to women, and exploring his identity; and his wish to work with an Indian woman if he goes into therapy.

Assessment

Jitu's presentation of himself – his persona – is harmonious with his chosen social role (consultant psychiatrist) and is an expression of his considerable ego strengths. These latter include his capacity to hold down a very responsible job, his parenting, his intellectual abilities, his powers of perceiving, observing, remembering, planning and reflecting. He also has a relationship with and a curiosity about his unconscious, which we know about from his reporting in one of his answers to me of a 'black cat dream':

> . . . six months or twelve months ago I dreamt of a black cat, in a sink, soiling itself. With me the observer. And in the distance an Indian man, standing in the background, wise, old. I dreamed that twice on different occasions. And I did discuss the dream with somebody, but we didn't get anywhere. But I was in the library and I was looking in a book of dreams and it said 'black cat – sometimes it denotes incipient depression'. Now I only discovered that after I became depressed. And I think the filthy cat, soiling the sink, ready to be washed away, is symbolical of that kind of thing. I think my depression is a good thing for me, although I don't like it. I think it is leading me like a light into an area which is part of me and which I must recognize.

His reserve in the interview situation suggests to me that he is primarily introverted and introspective, an attitude that he developed quite early in life, evidenced by occasional comments about sitting in trees or lying on his own in the sun. His superior function is thinking, which he recognizes – one that was encouraged at school and throughout his academic career. This implies that he has trouble with his feelings, many of which are unwelcome, and that these have ganged up on him, so to speak, in the form of depression. This I see as the Self's determination to redress in a compensatory way one-sided development in favour of the intellect.

Jitu's shadow seems to consist mainly of powerful feelings – sadness, rage, anger, loneliness – and possibly the loving feelings of excitement, joy, dependence and competitiveness. Many of these feelings, I suspect, are contained in the inner child, who is a very shadowy figure, banished to the realm of the shadow during the period of the father's illness and subsequent death, and further relegated to even greater depths at the time of the move from Uganda to Britain.

I sense some difficulty in the area of sexuality, and I surmise this partly from the lack of material about it (but this may be circumstantial and too early in the process) and partly from the complex constellation of people who carry in projection the contrasexual side of Jitu. This includes his mother, the African woman, his sisters and his Irish wife as well as his daughter(s). But in terms of Jitu's developmental stage, mid-life, this is just the time when I would expect a powerful projection on to a female figure such as *une femme inspiratrice* or *une femme fatale*. This is supported by his quest for 'feminine wisdom', which I think he may be seeking outside himself rather than discovering 'her' in his inner world. In exploring Jitu's early development, I am struck by a possible split in his feelings about his mother that might have occurred when Jitu was a toddler, and thus becoming more independent of his mother. It was at that time that he seems to have found his way to the African woman's quarters. This may have coincided with the birth of a younger sibling; however, this is conjecture, and would need to be tested during therapy. But this woman seems to have become the 'good' mother for a while, although the real and the surrogate mother seem somewhat undifferentiated.

Jitu's relationship with his father seems to have been very close – he was the 'favourite son' – and the father's death has had several consequences. At the time, because Jitu was only ten, his ego would have been overwhelmed by the intensity of affect, and it was in the period afterwards that Jitu developed his intellectual defences and capacities. A second result was the inner division into observer and participator, the observer usually in command and determined that once bitten, twice shy. After his father's death, Jitu seems to have become wary about close attachments to people of either sex and to have fostered a do-it-yourself psychology. He prefers solitary recreation and independence. This fear of abandonment may have contributed to him separating from his wife. Unresolved feelings about his father's death were probably instrumental in unleashing the grief over the death of Jitu's brother's death. But even then, the grief was experienced primarily in projection: 'I turned round and I saw Arvint, my brother, and it was sort of suffering personified; that was very upsetting'.

Another consequence of Jitu's father's death is I think a lack of opportunity to compete with and surpass his father. Although Jitu has reached the top of his profession, there is a feeling that he would have liked to have gone further: 'My idea of becoming a great expert and whatever, you know, has not been realized'. This is fairly typical of Oedipal depression and links to some problems with authority figures, as exemplified by a relationship, which he described in one of his replies to me, with a registrar who was sadistic. Furthermore, I can understand Jitu's occasional outburst of rage and anger as attempts to re-connect with his beloved father, who, by the way, seems shadowless and possibly idealized.

These Oedipal problems are also in evidence in an incident he told me about regarding another Irish girl and her ex-boyfriend, whom he observed hand-in-hand. But they are most in evidence, to my mind, in the fact of Jitu 'marrying out', which I might see as the living out of an incest taboo, possibly in relation to his mother/sister(s), and as a repeat of his attachment to the African woman.

From what I can gather, Jitu has always been interested in difference: difference within the family; difference between Indians and his African peers; difference between and within cultures; in how to be different in the sense of individuating, that is to say the process of separating out from the collective (be it family or culture) at the same time as adapting realistically to it; and in difference as it is manifested in the psychopathology of his suffering patients. He acknowledges that he is 'always worried about boundaries in that sense'. Elsewhere, he describes himself as 'a man at the watershed of life'. This all makes me think that he might be in a position where he feels neither fully in nor fully out of life, and this is endorsed by his feeling of meaninglessness, which is akin to a sense of futility, and his fear of death – death being an image of boundarylessness and possibly symbolizing a return to the negative aspect of the mother.

In summary, Jitu is a man in his mid-forties suffering from a sense of meaninglessness at mid-life, but actually depressed because of unresolved feelings in relation to the loss of his father before adolescence, all of which have left him cut off from large parts of himself. At a deeper level, there is evidence of a mother complex and some depression in relation to emotional deprivation at an early age. He has developed some schizoid defences, including splitting, projection and intellectualization. My own response to him has been one of being very moved by his account of his life, his increasing openness and his wish to understand himself and develop his inner life.

Therapeutic possibilities

Jitu is seeking therapy at an important developmental stage. He has great strengths as well as substantial achievements behind him. His disturbance is not such that therapy is likely to lead to disruptions in his professional life, which might affect his responsibilities towards his children. He is a member of a large extended family, whose support is probably always available, and whose members are likely to rally round him if he became quite depressed, which is probable. He has a wealth of inner resources, which include good-enough parents and significant others in the course of his development.

His motivation appears to be very strong, even to the extent that he was willing to put himself into what he considered initially to be a guinea-pig situation. Further evidence of his suitability for therapy lies in his willingness to uncover and experience hidden feelings, his awareness that his problems are emotional rather than practical, and in his curiosity about his unconscious. For instance, he not only reports a dream, but he also reports that he sought understanding of one of its images – the black cat – in a library book. Had I been the interviewer, I might have attempted to play with him about the dream, especially since it has stuck in his mind and is creating some fascination for him. Also, he can think about and respond to the idea that his depression may be teleological, purposive. Just as helpful is his capacity to contain the opposites. By this I mean that he has not taken sides with one of the poles of the archetypal image of the Wounded-Healer. He sees therapy as a means of helping himself (as Wounded) but also of enhancing his work (as Healer). He is similarly aware of the play of opposites when talking about how he has become the 'baddy' in his wife's counselling, and of the difficulties that such polarization is creating between him and his wife. All of this suggests to me the possibility of a favourable outcome and is strengthened to my mind by the clarity of his expectations of therapy.

As his prospective therapist, I foresee three areas of potential difficulty. In terms of typology, we would find each other difficult, since our superior functions are opposite. This can be very useful, since each of us will tend to stimulate each other's inferior function – thinking in my case, feeling in his. I anticipate also that there may be some language problem, not so much in terms of content as in terms of affect. For example, I have found from previous experience of working with clients whose mother-tongue is not English that it is necessary for me sometimes to ask them to speak their primary language in order to convey adequately to me the feeling attached to the content. And, thirdly, cultural differences between us may mean that I cannot relate on the basis of my usual assumptions – but that might not be such a bad thing.

A major consideration for me is Jitu's confusion about the sort of therapist he wants:

> C.P.: If you came into therapy, would you prefer to work with a man or a woman?

Jitu: I, I don't think that is important. You see, I wouldn't
say either a man or a woman. However, if I like a
particular man, I would prefer to work with that man;
or a woman. So it's not – it's the individual.

C.P.: If you came into therapy, would you prefer to work
with a therapist from your own or from this culture?

Jitu: Oh, I think in general I would say my culture. Because
they would understand my ideas. I think I would prefer
to work with an Indian female.

I will return to this question in the next section.

The course of therapy

I have implied that in my opinion Jitu could and probably would
benefit from analytic psychotherapy. But this conclusion, based on
quite a lengthy and thorough assessment process, leads to all sorts
of questions.

Jitu originally sought therapy for himself for quite specific reasons.
But in the course of his explorations he and his wife separated. That
is a momentous event in itself, not only for Jitu but also for the
whole family, including possibly Jitu's extended family. And I already have much evidence to suggest that change can be particularly disturbing to Jitu, and that his habitual way of coping with it
is to detach himself and let his 'observer' sub-personality take over.
I also know from experience that clients sometimes make these
major changes once a source of support and understanding has been
found, and that times of crisis can be times of optimal growth and
development if adequate containment is provided.

While my primary responsibility is to Jitu, I cannot think about
him in isolation. I need to know something about his perception of
the effects the separation is having on the children and on his wife.
Can a case be made out at this point for couple work to help the
partners to redefine their roles as parents, to offer a forum to contain
areas of conflict which might otherwise overspill into the children,
and to discuss the feelings about and practicalities of issues such as
access? Are the children showing signs of disturbance at home or
school? Do they need help? Is family therapy another possibility?

I do not have the sort of information that I need to arrive at
valid answers to these questions. But I do know that in my view it
is still possible for Jitu to embark on individual therapy as well as to
participate concurrently in couple or family therapy; and that this
combined approach may be the approach of choice, because it may

come closest to meeting the needs of all the members of the nuclear family at this point in time.

Before I knew that Jitu and his wife had separated, my thinking had gone along slightly different lines, such as these: Jitu can benefit greatly from a twice weekly analytic group as long as he is not an isolate (in terms of culture); preferably the group will be conducted by a man, and this will offer the possibility to Jitu of unblocking some of his feelings in relation to power, potency and authority, and some of his loving and hating feelings towards men. It is likely that many of the dynamics of Jitu's original family will be transposed onto the group, in which he can grapple with rivalry, jealousy and healthy competitiveness. The group will probably stimulate the emergence of powerful archetypal imagery and process, such as the Divine Child and migration respectively. His major defences – intellectualization and projection – will be greatly modified; the positive and negative aspects of the 'observer' will be disentangled; and he will have an enormous amount to contribute to the life of the group.

On the other hand, I can argue that what seems to have been lacking in Jitu's early upbringing is a close emotional relationship with a maternal figure, and that this developmental need can best be met by individual analytic psychotherapy with a female therapist. This is what Jitu has asked for, and I can see that what he wants and what he needs might neatly conflate.

Having reached that conclusion with Jitu, I then need to seek out an Indian female therapist who feels reasonably comfortable with the contrasexual masculine within herself. This is because during various periods of the therapy Jitu will need her to be paternal, penetrative and masculine as well as maternal, receptive and feminine.

If such a resource is not available, I will offer Jitu the possibility of working with me. I will explain that ideally we should meet at the same fixed three times a week with the possibility of increasing this frequency if the need arises. This aspect of the therapeutic alliance is important because the nature of Jitu's defences are such that a lesser frequency will probably give too much rein to the 'observer' and will militate against Jitu forming an attachment. I will not commit myself to a time limit, because when and how to end the therapy is part of the dialectic between him and me, and therefore something to be decided between us. Also, I wish to steer clear of notions of cure or anything prescriptive. I will explain that Jitu is free to use the time to explore whatever is on his mind, that part of our conversation will be about our relationship. I will have preliminary discussions with him about the use of the couch or the chair, since these are parts of the setting that I provide. Each has advantages and disadvantages, sometimes at different stages in the therapy. We will negotiate times, fees, understandings about cancellations and holiday periods; and I will ask his permission for me to write a brief letter to his GP (which I will show Jitu) informing him of Jitu's decision to start therapy.

Because of Jitu's current life situation, I expect that much of the material over the early weeks and months will centre around concerns about himself and his family, and that much of his energy will flow in those directions. I am also aware that his professional work is likely to be affected and that there may be times when he presents his own patients to whom he may be partially blinded because of his own emotional state. The intensity of his feelings between sessions may be such that I suggest that he writes, paints, draws or models them with the purpose of putting them outside himself and objectifying them, while at the same time sustaining a relationship with them. These can be brought to sessions for discussion in much the same way as dreams. If, however, this practice became habitual, I might suggest meeting more often.

From a theoretical point of view, I expect that, after some trust has been established between us and both of us feel sufficiently contained by the setting, the relationship and the process, Jitu will form a positive transference to me both developmentally and archetypally. From a developmental perspective, this will mean that positive aspects of Jitu's father will be projected onto me, and that this projection will evoke concomitant loving feelings in Jitu. From an archetypal perspective, I anticipate that I will be expected to incarnate the 'wise, old Indian man' of the black cat dream. These positive feelings and expectations will inevitably lead to disappointment and frustration and the emergence of negative feelings. The black cat dream is of importance here because to my mind it holds the possibility of assimilating and integrating the 'observer', the dark shitty side of Jitu and the Wise Old Man with the dream ego. If I do not retaliate against Jitu's anger, then we will be descending down a deepening spiral on which we will move in and out of positive and negative feelings towards each other. I will be attempting to understand these both reductively and teleologically; and they will include feelings towards Jitu's mother and other significant persons in his past.

Problem areas

I surmise that Jitu is essentially quite a private person. He himself owned up to feelings of shame when he lapsed into silence, and I have already alluded to the crippling effects of shame. I think it likely that there are in Jitu all sorts of feelings, phantasies, thoughts and impulses whose energy is potentially useful, if not vital, and that are encapsulated by shame. These are what Jungians refer to as contents of the Shadow, and the reclaiming of them is a major, if not *the* major, part of therapy. When these contents surface as a result of Jitu's psychic processes and my interpretations, Jitu will go into phases of resistance. His wish to understand himself and to be understood by me will be countered by a conservative impulse. This will be mirrored in me by a counter-resistance, a tendency to drift off into my own world or to feel very drowsy.

A second area of difficulty will be acute anxieties in relation to his attachment to me. His first primary attachment to a man was to his father; and his father died when he was ten; and his brother died several years later. These anxieties will be present to some degree throughout the therapy and may erupt towards the end. So we will need to transform the paradigm 'attachment = abandonment' to 'attachment can include separateness/togetherness'. This will mean facilitating the process of mourning for his father, Uganda, his brother, his marriage and his unfulfilled ambitions.

Third, I know that Jitu is searching for feminine Indian wisdom, and I suspect that he is searching for this outside himself. The two are not irreconcilable, but I anticipate that because I am a man Jitu will at some stage in the therapy project this feminine Indian wisdom on to an actual woman in the outside world. This might occur during a holiday break when feelings of abandonment could be assuaged by falling in love with a woman who tends to attract this sort of projection. At this stage, it will be necessary for me to try to hold the opposites of searching for meaning and giving way to the impulse to enact this alluring *coniunctio*. How this is handled will depend in part on how far Jitu has managed to separate psychologically from his wife. Were I a woman, I think this projection would be made on to me in the transference, where it would become erotically over-toned, very intense and of cardinal importance through its non-sexually enacted resolution.

This projection of the contrasexual archetype (the 'anima') will most likely drive the wedge further between Logos and Eros: the former residing in Jitu and comprising judgement, discrimination and insight; the latter residing in the recipient of the projection and comprising love, intimacy and relatedness. A goal of therapy from my point of view will be to get these two more balanced in relation to one another. But I suspect that this split will be constellated between us because of our different typology; and I am pretty sure that I shall find his intellectualization very irritating, as much as he will find my probing for feeling.

Finally, there are major cultural differences between me and Jitu, and these may include differences in values which could lead to impasse.

The problem areas are substantial but not untypical of any therapeutic endeavour. But I have had experience with clients for whom the therapeutic relationship has been a transitional relationship. The frustrations of this have been too great for both parties to work with, and the client has fallen for an external Messianic figure – and sometimes into contentment! The frustrations stem from the 'rule of abstinence' and the relative anonymity of the analyst, although the latter is generally overstated in the literature, because we convey so much of ourselves through every minute of the analytic hour. If I found myself in serious difficulties, I might seek supervision, possibly with an Indian analyst, and, if necessary, refer Jitu on to someone more suitable than myself.

An after-question: Why would such a private person, like Jitu, bare himself publicly to a group of therapists? And why would I agree to take part in this project? Exhibitionism/voyeurism is too easy an answer. Self-aggrandizement could be another piece of the jigsaw. Shopping around for the right sort of therapist could be another. But ultimately I think that all the participants in this venture (and principally the client) are seeking some proximity to the truth, in the hope that we can learn from one another, and further our understanding of which therapy can help whom at particular stages of life.

Criteria for successful outcome

Let me state at the outset that my own criterion for the successful outcome of analytic psychotherapy is that the client has the means and the tools to maintain an ongoing relationship with his or her unconscious. This may differ from my criterion for a successful outcome of psychotherapy, which to my mind involves the diminution or disappearance (although not through repression) of specific symptoms.

I am referring to a relationship between the ego and the Self, the latter of which is projected in the first instance on to the mother, who mediates the all-or-nothingness of archetypal contents and predispositions. This projection is re-played in the dynamics of the transference/counter-transference, and is then re-introjected by the client with an overlay of internalization. I am here differentiating between an introjection of a specific sub-personality of the analyst on the one hand, and an internalization of a relationship between a sub-personality of the client and a sub-personality of the analyst.

What is of vital importance to my mind in this dynamic is how analyst and client hold and transcend the opposites that threaten to blow apart the partnership of the client and the analyst. The growing ability to hold and transcend the opposites, which in Jitu's case might be temporarily (for example) those of transience and eternity, is for me perhaps the sole criterion for a successful outcome of analytic psychotherapy. The essential outcome of the work (and I cannot emphasize this enough) is the growing awareness of and the humility to the wisdom that has gone beyond. It is in this realm that I feel that Jitu and I may get on quite well. I am talking both of that which has to be embodied in its fullest sense through the re-working of developmental stages, and of that which, as Jung suggests, is a superior wisdom: that which is beyond the ken of client and therapist; that by which both are transformed.

I have now entered into the spiritual realm of therapy. This has to be put alongside its bodily aspects, which have to do with appetites, embodiment, incorporation, spitting out, biting, shitting, weeing, crying, choking, laughing, touching, smelling, being held (or not) and – not least in Jitu's case – beatification: he told me in response to a question about his relationship with his mother how she used to beautify the children's eyes at night with a type of mascara, and how she said to him, 'Look, your eyes are beautiful, because I used to do that for you'. What is 'that'? Here we run right into a major cultural difference. Is the boy made beautiful for the gods? Or is the boy made beautiful for his mother? What is the space between? Where is the meaning, and what is the demand for further development for client and therapist?

Jitu is seeking that which resides in himself. He is motivated, curious, insightful (not in the psychiatric sense) and courageous. I have the determination and commitment, to the best of my ability, to see us through the vicissitudes of change and disappointment. I shall require of him and of myself total obedience to the truth to myself and himself, that will lead us to that place where:

> On the seashore of endless worlds,
> children play . . .
>
> (Tagore)

Summary

Once upon a time, sadness and loneliness deluged his soul; and he longed for what was substantial, a 'somebeing', who was always there and whose arms enfolded him, supported him and stopped him in his headlong rush into the pitfalls of life. They had danced together on the chessboard of life, and he had taught him the richness of defeat, the failing that led to questing, the 'unlimited ladder of emancipation'.

There is nothing Jitu does not know; and there is much that I do not know. Between us is the possibility of discovery through time, space and relationship; through faith, doubt and courage. The branches of the tree need only to look to their roots – and these include my own.

As a classical Jungian analyst, I feel that my therapeutic approach as well as my theoretical understanding of human development lends my analytic technique to the dilemmas that Jitu is facing in his life at present. But he may disagree, and our mutual bewilderment may be part of his individuation, as well as of mine.

Further reading

Jung, C.G. (1963). *Memories, Dreams and Reflections*. London: Collins/ Routledge and Kegan Paul.

NEIL ROTHWELL

8

THERAPY FROM A BUDDHIST PERSPECTIVE

The therapist

In this chapter, I describe the way my practice and understanding as a Buddhist informs my therapeutic work, in this case with Jitu. I am a clinical psychologist and have, until recently, worked with adults with a wide spectrum of mental health problems in the NHS. This includes people diagnosed as psychotic and those who have long-term contact with psychiatric services as well as people referred from their GP with such problems as anxiety and depression.

Buddhism is a way of directly perceiving Truth through experience, and meditation is the central form of practice for achieving this. The form of meditation I practice is called 'serene reflection meditation' (Jiyu-Kennett *et al.* 1989). This essentially involves just sitting while allowing thoughts to arise naturally and then letting go of them. For example, if one hears a car outside, that is simply perceived. It may be that the mind then goes off on a tangent thinking about the cost of buying a new car or whatever. If this happens, the mind is brought back to the stillness and awareness of the meditation. All mental activity is dealt with in the same way. Besides formal sitting periods, meditation is carried through into everyday life by maintaining the same inner stillness. Whatever comes up in the mind is accepted without judgement and without trying to clutch at thoughts and ideas. In doing this, one comes to know that the stillness that underlies all the surface 'noise' does, in fact, permeate everything. In Buddhism, this is sometimes referred to as the Unborn and the manifestation of this within oneself as the Buddha Nature. This is the source of compassion and peace.

Viewed in this way, psychological difficulties are the result of trying to reject or suppress thoughts or feelings that are regarded as bad while clinging on to those seen as desirable. Naturally, many thoughts and emotions are, by their nature, disturbing; but by neither clinging to nor avoiding them, their energy becomes spent and they simply dissolve. I am aware that this is simpler to describe than it is to do and one only has to meditate for a short while to see how well-ingrained the clinging/aversion habit is. In fact, by clearly seeing the manifestations of this habit in the mind, one is already beginning to release oneself from it. In this way, the healing process can start at this very moment.

In Buddhism, it is said that all activity is permeated with meditation and it is not necessary for a person to practise serene reflection meditation formally in order to begin to free themselves from mental suffering. Psychotherapy is another means of moving in this direction. Talking about problems can be a useful way of opening them up and thereby letting go of them. As a therapist, I feel I can best help this by maintaining a meditative mind myself during therapy sessions. This entails being aware of what is happening in the therapeutic session. Looked at objectively, individual therapy consists of two people talking to each other, both having a flow of inner thoughts and feelings. In order to be effective, I need to be fully aware of what I am experiencing and understand as clearly as possible what the other person is experiencing. A therapeutic model that describes this well is person-centred therapy, developed by Carl Rogers (1961). This focuses on the therapist's attitude and states that a therapist will be effective to the extent to which they can be warm, genuine and empathic towards the client. Warmth is sometimes also described as respect and, for me, entails a recognition of the client's Buddha Nature and that deep down lies the innate ability to overcome all problems. Genuineness refers to the therapist having the mind of meditation and being open to whatever is happening inside himself or herself in each moment. Empathy describes the therapist's attempt to understand the world as the client sees it. It is impossible to do this fully, but the attempt to do this on the part of the therapist is an important expression of the compassionate desire to help, which the client will perceive at some level, and also helps the therapist to behave in a way which is constantly attuned to the client's needs. Person-centred therapy does not, strictly speaking, prescribe what the therapist should do during therapy, and I often find it useful to use specific techniques within this context. However, I see these person-centred principles as the irreducible foundation of effective therapy and the research literature on psychotherapy generally supports this.

Further information requested and assessment

Comments on the initial session

In this section, I record my reactions to what Jitu has said in the first session. This is the equivalent of my assessment. I do this as both a clinical psychologist and a Buddhist. It may be apparent from what I have said already that it is not easy to separate these, although I do not explicitly use Buddhist terms in therapy.

Jitu starts by describing the frame of mind in which he is coming to therapy and what he is hoping to achieve from it. Both these have important implications for the course of therapy and I will consider them in more detail later. In the second paragraph, he immediately draws attention to his childhood. The past can leave a legacy which affects the person's current life; in this case, speaking about it can be a means of letting go of it and thereby becoming free of it. For Jitu, the past has left a legacy of 'deep feelings of sadness or complexity or ambivalence' which he would like to understand better. Jitu then goes on, for the first time, to talk about the death of his father. He implies that the reason this is still affecting him so much is that he did not allow himself to experience fully the feelings of grief at the time of the death – that is, he suppressed them. Note that he mentions this area quite briefly at this early stage of the session but returns to it later. This is a very characteristic and natural part of therapy, which can be seen as a cyclical process. Talking about the loss quite briefly opens the area up in his mind, enabling him to explore it at greater depth later.

The topic he then moves to is culture in two particular manifestations – coming to Britain from Uganda and marrying an Irish Protestant woman. The status of these differs from the loss of his father in that they both are a continuing part of his everyday external reality. This leads him to contemplate the interface between past and present, of how he is one particular person living at a particular time. He experiences a feeling of insignificance, a form of humility, which is often the expression of a spiritual yearning; indeed, Jitu talks about this within himself. What he says about it is interesting:

> I would expect a therapist to perhaps tackle that at some stage. I would expect that sort of interaction. If it wasn't it would be a terrible . . . gap in the relationship for me.

One thing that I find valuable about being a Buddhist is that it allows me to feel comfortable discussing these issues when they arise in therapy. Psychological theory is concerned with objective knowledge, and cannot adequately address the transcendent and experiential nature of spiritual awareness. The therapist is therefore thrown back on his or her own personal experience.

From this Jitu talks about traversing the middle stage of his life and coming to terms with mortality. This is an expression of another spiritual gateway, the awareness of impermanence. Everything is transitory in an ultimate sense. Perhaps another aspect of his father's death is that it first made him aware of this. In the same way, his own life is impermanent and he considers the prospect of going through his life without finding meaning, having not experienced spiritual realization himself. He identifies that one of the blocks to this realization is a tendency to divide the suffering he perceives in others (e.g. violence) from his own suffering. This expresses an intuitive understanding that the Buddha Nature is one and undivided.

Given a choice of topics to expand on, Jitu chooses dying, specifically the death of his father. He gives a moving account of his father's deterioration and his own sense of loss. He clearly felt a lot of inner pain at that time and this also seems to have been the start of his habit of not allowing himself to fully experience feelings for fear they will overwhelm him. This is understandable enough, given his closeness to his father, but this tendency has become long-term and something he would like to be free of. After Jitu talks about his family and particularly the death of his brother, the interviewer focuses on what may be holding back Jitu from getting in touch with his feelings. In psychoanalytic terms, this is exploring his defences and is a common therapeutic strategy. Another possibility at this point would tend to draw attention to Jitu's strengths, for example, by asking what has enabled him to cope with the considerable number of deaths in his life. This is a solution-focused strategy based on the premise that by inviting clients to talk about themselves more positively, they will as a result start to think about themselves in a way that challenges their own sense of incompleteness. Solution-focused therapy is an approach which is described further below.

After a discussion about separateness, Jitu makes the following comment:

> I think it may be something to do with being overwhelmed
> by the present in a sense, although I do not know what
> present I am talking about or where that comes from.

This has a strongly meditative flavour, pointing to the way unresolved distress can manifest itself when a person is still. Jitu describes the distress in terms of 'being overwhelmed'. As outlined above, fully experiencing the distress (while not getting too fascinated by it) is an important and necessary part of becoming free of it. Also in this comment, he expresses humility regarding his lack of understanding of what is going on here. This is an expression of what in Buddhism is termed *beginner's mind*. Beginner's mind is the essence of spiritual awareness and describes the open mind, free from fixed preconceptions, with which a person can approach each new situation and indeed each new moment. This is equally applicable to a person coming to a psychotherapist for the first time and is a key factor in therapeutic change. The very act of attending for therapy is an expression of openness. I feel that, whatever the person's motivation in other aspects, if they have the willingness to attend sessions, then they have sufficient motivation to do useful therapeutic work.

Jitu returns to the issue of motivation in therapy a short while later, questioning whether the intensity of his feelings at the present time is sufficient to justify his exploring them in therapy. This is a very pertinent question and one which a person considering therapy needs to think about carefully. The role of therapy and counselling can be regarded as releasing oneself from unresolved psychological conflicts. For a person who has, for example, tended to suppress a problem or aspects of it, this release can be found by talking through issues. At the same time, part of being alive is the experience of unpleasant feelings, and it is ultimately empowering for individuals to be able to face up to, and let go of, these feelings themselves. I hope to help Jitu move towards this in the course of therapy.

Following this, Jitu explicitly addresses the area of spirituality in terms of centring oneself. In talking about this, he links the sense of being connected with behaving ethically. He uses the term 'dharma', which is a term referring to Hindu or Buddhist teaching. In making this link, he does, in fact, go to the heart of Buddhist teaching on morality. This teaching is embodied in the Buddhist precepts, the essence of which is:

> Cease from evil
> Do only good
> Do good for others

By acting in accordance with what one knows deep down to be for the best, it is possible to remain in harmony with the Buddha Nature and know the unity of all things. Conversely, doing harmful acts creates a sense of separateness and isolation. For example, the act of stealing generally entails cutting oneself off from the suffering experienced by the victim of the theft. This attempt to separate creates inner tension. It has been said previously that connection is a major theme of Jitu's interview; and in this section he identifies the key role of right behaviour and thinking in maintaining the sense of connectedness. Of course, this applies equally to the therapist. No matter how 'stuck' the client may appear to be, it is important for the therapist not to act or speak in a violent way in an attempt to make the client open up.

My further questions

On the basis of the initial session, I asked Jitu four more questions, which I here record, with their answers in full. In reading them, it may be useful to bear in mind that this is not a dialogue in the normal sense, as I asked *all* the questions before receiving the reply from Jitu to any one of them.

Question 1: One thing that strikes me about your account of your father's death is the contrast between the warm, loving man you sat with in his bedroom and the frail, weak man struggling up the stairs and gradually fading away. Can you say more about the feelings this brings up in you?

I think it was the first experience of illness and death. It was the first feeling, if you like, of foreboding or danger. I was certainly aware of it having affected a friend of mine, yet it was a distant experience, it was like a news event. You just read it and, oh, you've heard about it and you excluded it, you didn't let it register within you. This might be a lot of denial, if you like, or a very acute fear of such things, that the merest whiff of it would be enough to just close the feelings down. But when it happened to you, the same reaction occurred. I think the first thing that you feel is, you're not sure where you are, really. It is a question of a sort of re-orientation. I would say, going back to that time, it's like a new experience. Hitherto not experienced – I'm going back to when I was ten, eleven – one didn't know what one felt. At that moment I decided I wouldn't feel. It was not conscious, it just happened. So, if you stay with that experience, I think it's indescribable. Because it's like standing on the edge of a precipice, not knowing what is going to be, and nobody there available to you, to explain the terrain. I think that's exactly how it felt.

Question 2: You make a number of references to blocks within yourself, for example 'the will to negate emotion', perhaps because of an underlying fear, which you also mention. It sounds as though working through these blocks will involve confronting the fear. How do you feel about that?

The feelings are mixed. Certainly they are not clear, but the feelings are mixed. It is of the rage within me. Rage is destructive, whereas anger is not. But the other feeling, often in therapy, of breaking down, doesn't worry me so much. I think rage worries me more than any other feeling.

Question 3: One effect of the past events and transitions seems to be that it brings up a feeling of not knowing, which is closely related to the vulnerability you speak about. It is as though your previous understanding of life begins to fall away at these times, and you are left confronting your experience in the raw, which is both threatening and exciting at the same time. Is this how it seems to you?
I understand this question very clearly. I think that in terms of transition it is mixed, it must be mixed because it is not familiar – by definition, there is an unknown in it. I would not use the term 'not knowing'. You have skills, techniques, for dealing with transitions or learning from transitions. There are inner experiences and outer experiences, and so that thing is there, and one can tolerate it. I don't think it has ever been such that I have felt totally unable to tolerate it.

Question 4: I get the impression that the vulnerability is, in a way, closely linked to your questions about meaning and enlightenment. The vulnerability seems to lead to an awareness of simply being here in the moment. Is that your perception also?
There is an obvious need to be aware. Certainly I don't see it that way. But that doesn't mean it wasn't like that or isn't like that.

Comments on the questions and answers

From the outset of therapy, I see my role as establishing an open-ended dialogue with the client in a way that facilitates the client's inner development. I therefore trust information (or my asking questions) to arise as needed (e.g. when the client feels ready to say it). For this reason, the invitation to ask Jitu supplementary questions presented something of a challenge, as I did not feel the need to obtain specific information in order to make a formulation or diagnosis. Instead, I asked questions which I hoped would point to the mind of meditation, bearing in mind Buddhism's teaching that this is something we all recognize intuitively.

In the original session, when Jitu is invited to select one of several topics he has raised for further exploration, he chooses his relationship with, and death of, his father. I therefore chose this as the starting point for my questions. His choice interested me because, besides being something he feels deeply about, it once again points to the experience of impermanence, something he seems to be keenly aware of in this context. This is naturally a source of grief for him and presumably the reason he decided to mention it was because there are still unanswered questions in his mind about it. This is inevitably speculative on my part and I would want to check my understanding of this with him if we decide to meet. Part of the grieving process is the more or less acknowledged understanding that because everything is impermanent, there is nothing that can be held onto to provide a sense of security. Jitu answers this directly and honestly by talking about the fear he felt and his attempts to protect himself from this fear by shutting off from it. Towards the end of his first answer he describes an experience which often arises in meditation: standing at the threshold of the unknown. Facing impermanence head on leads to a letting go of the things one clings to for security and entering the Buddha Mind – experiencing each moment anew. This can, indeed, be a frightening feeling and Jitu aptly uses the metaphor of standing on the edge of a precipice without knowing whether or not it is safe to jump. It is not surprising, then, that most of us tend to shrink back from the precipice at first and try to find something in our mind or in our activity that we know and feel safe with.

In the second question I take up this point explicitly, asking Jitu about the prospect of jumping over the precipice – that is, confronting the fear. He suggests in his answer that his rage is the object of his fear. I take from this that he tends to suppress rage if it threatens to arise in case it overwhelms him and becomes destructive. Certainly, in Buddhism, getting caught up in anger and rage is seen as a cause of suffering that will increase the tendency to future outbursts of rage. It is the 'getting caught up' which is the problem, and the way this is dealt with in meditation is to allow oneself to fully experience it and accept it without self-judgement and without trying to justify it. This is in contrast to some therapeutic approaches which advocate 'expressing' the anger (e.g. shouting at someone) in order to 'let it out'. From the perspective of meditation, this runs the risk of getting caught up with emotions by acting on them rather than just letting them be. This is not to deny that anger may be so intense at times that the person may feel unable to keep it to himself or herself; it is just that one needs to go beyond this stage in order to fully overcome anger.

The third question is an attempt to draw attention to the meditative mind and reframe it as a positive state rather than simply the absence of familiar psychological props. Jitu responds initially by acknowledging this. He then refers to strategies he uses to deal with transitions, implying that letting go of these strategies might lead to him becoming overwhelmed by his emotions.

It is apparent to me in retrospect that my four questions move in a particular direction, starting with an awareness of suffering, moving on to factors which may prevent the suffering being let go of, then describing the nature of meditation (although I do not use that term). Finally, in the fourth question, I suggest that his direct, meditative awareness of his vulnerability may be the gateway to the spiritual realization he is seeking. Because I did not have Jitu's response to each question before asking the next one, these questions were speculative: I have the sense now from his responses that the questions are gradually drifting away from where he is at. This is particularly evident in his response to the last question, although he maintains an open mind to the possibility I suggest.

Therapeutic possibilities

I see the essential task in assessing Jitu as gaining an empathic understanding of his difficulties in order to act in a way that will be most helpful to him. One set of specific techniques I often use are those of solution-focused therapy (de Shazer 1988). I find this useful because it is very practical, and therefore can be readily taught and implemented, yet I believe it is based firmly on person-centred principles. The basic approach is to establish what the person wishes to achieve from therapy and then to help them to identify ways in which they are already starting to meet these aims. The purpose of this is to draw the person's attention to their own strengths and resources rather than only their weaknesses. People coming for therapy very commonly have a sense of inadequacy and are acutely aware of their negative aspects. A second useful aspect of a solution-focused approach is that, by defining clearly what the goals of therapy are, it becomes possible to identify when these goals have been achieved and therefore when therapy will end. I prefer to see therapy as a time-limited activity which can act as a catalyst to enable a person to transcend a particular situation or move in a new direction. It may be that some people find it helpful to have therapy at several different times in their life. At the same time, it is useful to bear in mind that there are many forms of personal development other than counselling and psychotherapy, some of which go considerably deeper.

It is important to establish clearly at the outset whether a new client does in fact wish to have any therapy at all. In Jitu's case, he does say at the start of the initial interview that he would like to see a therapist. The only time I work with people who do not attend of their own accord is when they are there at the request of a third party. This is the case, for example, when someone is compulsorily detained in hospital under the Mental Health Act. In this instance, it may be possible to frame the goals in terms of what needs to be different in order to satisfy the third party that treatment (or compulsory detention) is no longer necessary (the GP who refers a person to the psychology department would not be classed as a third party in this way, as the person will have voluntarily taken the step of seeking help from the GP in the first instance).

A key feature of a solution-focused approach is that the criteria for success in therapy are effectively set by the clients themselves. In a NHS setting, people are often referred to a psychologist with a clearly defined problem area. It is usually fairly straightforward for clients to translate this into goals. The length of therapy is then determined by when the goals have been achieved. Very often, the goal may not be fully achieved in the course of therapy itself, but the person will have made a change in the direction they are taking which, if continued, is likely to lead to the goal being achieved. In this event, I may suggest ending the sessions, with the proviso that the person can contact me again in the future if they wish. It can be seen from this that there is a relationship between the initial setting of goals and the length of therapy.

Jitu describes his therapeutic aims in general terms in the interview. In order to clarify goals, it is usually necessary to question the person carefully, and this is something I will want to address with Jitu at our first meeting. However, at the start of the interview, Jitu outlines two areas he hopes to be addressed in therapy. One of these relates to his sphere of work. He hopes that being in therapy will enhance his effectiveness as a psychiatrist working with people in need. It is likely to be beneficial for any therapist to have the experience of being in therapy. As well as the self-understanding aspect, it can make empathizing with clients considerably easier. Thus, although Jitu does not have a circumscribed problem area in the way that an NHS client typically does, a need for therapy does, perhaps, arise because of the nature of his work.

He has identified his second general goal as understanding himself and seeking meaning in life. It seems that what he is saying, in effect, is that he would see therapy as a means for taking him further along the path of inner development. The Buddhist view sees everyone as being on this path; even activities such as chasing wealth or power are ultimately an attempt to find peace or self-acceptance. The practical question which arises for Jitu is how far should he use therapy as a means of going along this path; in other words, what are the criteria for his finishing therapy? This will be something to explore in my first session with him; it may be possible to translate this into something quite specific. If not, I may suggest the possibility of having a fixed number of sessions, say six, and then reviewing the situation.

The next issue to explore in our first session is when and how often future sessions will occur. In the initial interview, Jitu says he is 'feeling relatively OK' at the present time. It is at more vulnerable times in the past that he has very much wanted help. It will be worth considering, in the light of this, whether he wishes to start therapy at this time or whether he would prefer to contact me at a later time when he feels the need for help. In this latter instance I would, of course, endeavour to see him as soon as possible after he had contacted me. It is clear from what Jitu is saying here that his motivation to seek help is directly proportional to the amount of distress he is feeling. This is a very common experience. One of the major catalysts for looking more deeply at one's life is suffering. This is made explicit in Buddhism, with a recognition of suffering's existence being seen as the start of the path to liberation. It follows from this that suffering can have great value and this is one of the reasons that Buddhism does not see the world as fundamentally divided into good and evil. When seen with the non-judgemental eyes of meditation, all experiences can teach us. At the same time, the clarity that this produces helps us to see clearly ways in which we ourselves inadvertently cause suffering, thereby providing us with the opportunity to prevent future suffering. This is a process which can also take place in effective psychotherapy.

The frequency of sessions is another issue which I would see as largely being determined by Jitu himself. Very often, clients choose to meet surprisingly infrequently given a free choice. This fits in with a view of therapy as consisting of a series of free-standing events (i.e. individual sessions), each one of which can act as a catalyst for change in the client. For example, a person may see the possibility of moving in a new direction in their life as a result of a particular therapy session. This may take some time for them to become used to and to start tentatively putting into practice. Less frequent sessions can allow the space for this. On a practical level, it can be easier for people to take time out of their work if the appointments are spaced out.

The course of therapy

I have described in a very general way some of the areas which will affect the way therapy with Jitu will work out in practice. I find it a lot easier to describe general features of the process of therapy than it is to detail what the content is likely to be. This is not a barrier to a successful outcome. The aim of my therapeutic approach is to provide a safe and compassionate space in which Jitu will feel free to move in whichever direction he wishes. He may want to expand on some of the themes described in the initial session or he may raise some completely new and unexpected theme. My approach is very much a 'here and now' one, in the sense that I am happy to accept whatever Jitu chooses to share with me. The mind of meditation is sometimes described as one of all-acceptance, and I find that by maintaining this mind myself the client is often able to get in touch with the meditative process within himself or herself.

As previously stated, meditation is a process of seeing directly and for this reason I will not try to analyse or interpret what Jitu is saying. To analyse an experience is to create an intellectual structure which filters the perception of it. This can have its uses, but psychological problems often arise out of a tendency to use the intellect to try and manipulate direct experience. Jitu gives a good example of this in the initial session when he describes himself as being over-intellectualized, describing this as 'a defence of some sort'. He talks about this in the context of 'the will to negate emotion', so it seems that the intellectualization is an attempt to push away unwanted feelings.

Central to my therapeutic approach is a recognition of the Buddha Nature and its ability to overcome all obstacles. This translates into a humanistic model, placing great emphasis on Jitu's natural potential for growth. For this reason, I will be happy to allow the therapy to unfold in its own way. It can be the case, in some instances, that what unfolds is the need for a specific therapeutic technique. This in no way undermines the growth process provided it is carefully based on an empathic understanding of the person's need and the flexibility to change direction if necessary is maintained. Jitu seems happy to explore things in an open-ended way and it may be that 'the gentle art of listening' will be my main activity with him.

A solution-focused technique I may adopt with Jitu is the use of the 'break'. These days I usually make notes during a session, specifically to record the positive achievements and coping ability that the client mentions, perhaps in passing. During the session I draw out and amplify these abilities by focusing attention on them and exploring them further. Towards the end of the session, I often take a short break by leaving the room, explaining to the client that I wish to gather my thoughts together in order to feed back my impressions of our discussion. I use this break to highlight about four or five positive points and achievements, which I point out to the client after the break immediately before ending the session. The break and feedback often has quite an impact on the client. More and more I am discovering the importance of positive feedback as a powerful agent of change. One may think that this may lead to arrogance in some cases, but I have never found this to be so. Arrogance is a defensive reaction and as such is incompatible with the openness with which people generally come to therapy. Jitu is at the 'successful' end of the client spectrum in terms of the position he has achieved in life, yet he can still describe experiences of confusion, meaninglessness and being withdrawn; such feelings can occur whatever a person's external position. This would therefore seem to be an appropriate approach to take with Jitu. The only time I find difficulty using this approach is when a person is unremittingly negative or if their thinking processes are very confused; but neither of these is the case with Jitu.

Is there anything about solution-focused therapy that is specifically Buddhist? At one level the answer is 'no', in that all therapies are based on a compassionate desire to help: it is simply that they approach problems from different directions. As they are all manifestations of the Unborn, they all express a useful teaching from which one can learn. At the same time, it is a common experience in Buddhism that different aspects of the Truth come into focus as one's understanding matures. This means that one must be willing to let go of previous conceptions of reality if a deeper perception arises. This applies to both the therapist, in terms of their understanding of therapy, and the client, in terms of their perception of their problems. In this sense, our understanding is always provisional. Solution-focused therapy appeals to me because it seeks to bring about change by this very means of changing a person's perception of problems, but in a way which is respectful of their current understanding – it is not the 'expert' therapist trying to impose change from outside. Equally important is that I have found it to be very effective. Other Buddhist therapists may take different approaches (see, for example, Claxton 1986). It is also relevant to note here that there is an interaction between the personality of the therapist and the therapeutic model used; in other words, one therapist may be more effective with one model and a different therapist with another.

Problem areas

It has been said that client 'resistance' is a sign of therapist inflexibility. The main challenge in this way is to be constantly in tune with

Jitu in order to be able to make contact with him whatever he is talking about. In general, the things which tend to affect adversely the quality of the help I can offer are inattention and judgementalism. Inattention can occur, for example, if I am tired or am worried about some external concern. Tiredness inevitably reduces mental agility, and I try to maintain a reasonable sleep pattern as far as is practicable. Worry is one aspect of the mind's tendency to attach itself to mental objects and is best dealt with by awareness, since becoming aware of the worrying train of thought allows me to gently let go of it and come back to the task in hand. Judgementalism seems to be an endemic aspect of the Western psyche and can also be best dealt with by awareness. It is possible that I may find myself becoming judgemental with Jitu, but if I look at this carefully I will almost certainly find that underlying this is a negative judgement about some aspect of myself. In other words, Jitu will be evoking a reaction in me that I do not regard as 'good'. The point is frequently made that the Buddha is not some external deity who stands in judgement over us. But past conditioning can run deep and it is not always easy to accept this. It is therefore important for therapists to maintain a compassionate stance towards both themselves and their clients. Such a stance is possibly the most powerful aspect of therapy, as it also allows the client to abandon the self-criticism that is at the heart of so many psychological problems. This comes about through the client talking about sensitive areas, and finding that the therapist is accepting of these and does not deliver the censure which may be unconsciously feared.

Criteria for successful outcome

I stated earlier that the goals of therapy will be set by Jitu himself and I see the meeting of these goals as the essential criteria for successful therapy. As a therapist, I am most concerned with Jitu's perception of the usefulness of therapy and I am also guided by Carl Rogers' observations on the process of client movement in therapy. Broadly speaking, he said that clients tend to move away from façades, rigid self-expectations and trying to always please others, and towards an acceptance of the complexity and flow of their own experience. This is essentially another way of describing the movement of meditation, although Rogers did not use this term. With Jitu, as with any client, I am likely to find myself intuitively encouraging and supporting any moves he makes in this direction.

Having said this, movement in therapy is an extremely individual process and I feel it is important not to impose any arbitrary constraints on the direction Jitu may wish to take. Indeed, he may feel that his initial goals themselves become constraining and may therefore wish to modify or abandon them. Goal-setting can be empowering because it enables clients to set their own agenda in therapy rather than passively accepting the expertise of the therapist; at the same time, it is only a tool which can be used or dispensed with according to the needs of the situation.

Optimism is an essential quality of an effective therapist and one which arises naturally out of respect for the client and faith in their Buddha Nature. Jitu comes to our sessions with a good deal of frankness and the willingness to look with clear eyes at the experiences which have made him what he is now. I am hopeful that, if he wishes to have some sessions of therapy with me at the present time, he is likely to find a benefit from them.

Conclusion

It should be apparent from what I have written that I regard openness and the willingness to attend for therapy as major criteria determining its usefulness, which is why I have laid so much emphasis on it at an early stage. I will be seeing Jitu in slightly different circumstances than I normally see clients. This has caused me to reflect on my general approach to therapy and the way I will adapt it with him. It has also been very instructive for me to try and make explicit the way in which Buddhism underlies my therapeutic approach. Normally, this is a rather intuitive and underlying process, which none the less influences my understanding of therapy. To articulate it in writing in terms of a particular person has enabled me to look at my practice from a different perspective than I would normally take.

Further reading

Claxton, G. (ed.) (1986). *Beyond Therapy: The Impact of Eastern Religions on Psychological Theory and Practice*. London: Wisdom.

de Shazer, S. (1988). *Clues: Investigating Solutions in Brief Therapy*. London: Norton.

Jiyu-Kennett, Rev. P.T.N.H. and Monks of the Order of Buddhist Contemplatives (1989). *Serene Reflection Meditation*. Mount Shasta, CA: Shasta Abbey Press. (Available from Throssel Hole Priory Bookshop, Tel. 01434 345204.)

Rogers, C.R. (1961). *On Becoming a Person: A Therapist's View of Psychotherapy*. London: Constable.

Acknowledgements

Thanks to the Rev. Master Daishin Morgan, John Higgon, Myra Rothwell and Michael Sheldon for commenting on an earlier draft of the manuscript.

9

DIANA WHITMORE

PSYCHOSYNTHESIS PSYCHOTHERAPY

The therapist

My own training in psychology was just the opposite of Jitu's academic career. Although I have a Masters degree in education, I have no academic credentials in psychology. My professional training in psychotherapy began in 1969 at the Esalen Institute, the Californian Centre for the Development of Human Potential. There I trained in Humanistic Psychology, primarily in Gestalt Therapy, and I discovered Psychosynthesis. Later I furthered my studies in Psychosynthesis both at the University of California and in Italy with its founder, Dr Roberto Assagioli.

Since 1972, psychosynthesis has been the therapeutic approach that I practise, and in which I run professional training. Psychosynthesis provides me with a broad perspective of human development based upon unifying one's personality expression with a deeper source of purpose and direction in life, the transpersonal Self. This is seen as the integrating principle of the personality and as a source of wisdom, inspiration, unconditional love, and the will to meaning and service. As a multidimensional and open system, psychosynthesis has provided me with the psychospiritual framework which integrates and makes available to me most other forms and practices of psychotherapy. It is an 'open system' which gives ample space for my own development and creative expression. In short, I have not felt limited nor dogmatized by this approach.

Psychosynthesis was created by the Italian psychiatrist Roberto Assagioli (1888–1974). Soon after having completed a psychoanalytic training, and having been considered by Freud and Jung as a representative of psychoanalysis in Italy in 1910, he broke away from Freudian orthodoxy and gradually created his own approach.

Psychosynthesis is a unified conception of human development and an organized system of techniques that can be applied in the fields of psychotherapy, education and medicine. It is concerned with the realization of human potential, and at the same time with harmonization of all elements of the personality so as to avoid unbalanced growth. Among the methods used are creative visualization, free drawing, the training of the will, physical expression, dis-identification, meditation, interpersonal and groupwork.

A dichotomy can occur between the insights of mystics and creative individuals of all cultures and the findings of contemporary Western psychology. The latter tends to have as its primary goal the creation of a normal, fully functioning personality, but it may ignore the higher realms of consciousness. Values, meaning, peak experiences and the unquantifiable, ineffable essence of human life are often not addressed, yet these are the very things to which spiritually oriented people aspire. Psychosynthesis attempts to acknowledge and harmonize both these realms. On the psychological level it aims to build a personality that is free from emotional blocks, has command over all its functions and has a clear awareness of its own centre. On the transpersonal level, it enables a person to explore those regions full of mystery and wonder beyond our ordinary awareness, which we call the superconscious – the wellspring of higher intuitions, inspirations, ethical imperatives and states of illumination. This exploration has as its context the Self, our true essence beyond all masks and conditions.

The first step in psychosynthesis is the attainment of a certain level of self knowledge, the ability to move within one's inner world. For this to happen we must first enter into relationship with that inner universe of feelings, memories and images from which our extroverted society tends to alienate us. We can then continue the exploration by contacting those aspects of ourselves which we have relegated to the unconscious because we found them too painful to experience, or because they conflict with the conscious image we have of ourselves, or with the dominant cultural norms.

If this first task of self knowledge is undertaken in the right way (avoiding the danger of losing oneself in a labyrinth of endless investigations), we become aware that within us there are many more or less conscious aspects, roles and attitudes with which from time to time we identify ourselves, to the point of forgetting or repressing the rest of our personality. When we identify in this way with one part of ourselves, we become ruled and enslaved by it. We can be dominated by anxiety or depression, or by a prejudice or an ambition. We at times experience ourselves to be prisoners of oppressive psychological patterns which appear to be beyond our control.

Such identification is a universal process which can be reversed by its opposite, 'dis-identification', an attitude whereby we consciously detach ourselves from all the various aspects of our personality, thus discovering our true 'I', our centre. This experience of being centred can give us a clear impression of inner freedom, and helps us to perceive who we really are.

Further information requested

Given that psychosynthesis does not hold a normative definition of a healthy and fully functioning individual, a high value is placed on inner freedom and upon the client gaining mastery over his psychological state. My task is to help Jitu enlarge his possibilities and choices. This freedom of choice will enable him to live as he deems meaningful and worthwhile, and hopefully will enable him to become increasingly responsible for his inner development and outer behaviour. Psychosynthesis fully recognizes that those seeking therapy need to accept and address their negative and destructive elements and integrate their personality. A psychosynthesis therapist approaches the client with a belief in the client's capacity to understand life, to make choices and to transcend apparent limitations. Jitu's problems and difficulties are not seen as the result of mere inadequacy or childhood conditioning, but as challenges and opportunities for growth.

From Michael Jacobs' initial interview with Jitu, my first concern was Jitu's motivation for therapy. It is with this initial motivation in mind that I see both the future direction of work and its potential for success. By success, I mean that the client knows what the purpose of the work will be for him and that his therapeutic goals have been both defined and met. Every client comes to the initial interview with a presenting issue and a particular motivation. My questions to Jitu had the aim of helping him to formulate, clarify and define them, while broadening his awareness. I wanted to enable him to develop a positive intention for the direction of the work.

I immediately noticed a noble motivation being expressed by Jitu. He said he wanted to see a therapist for two broad categories: personally, to better understand himself, and also as 'someone who is looking after other people'. He was insightful when he said, 'I realize that it is essentially understanding myself, but only in understanding myself may I understand other people'. This is already a conscious intention which goes beyond mere alleviation of suffering or wanting to feel better. Jitu also recognizes a need for meaning in life, linked to both the above areas. This indicated to me that Jitu would be open to exploring both the personal dimension of his life and the transpersonal area of meaning, as well as the more spiritual elements of life.

Jitu said that at the moment he was feeling 'relatively okay', but that 'at other moments there is another place in him that feels vulnerable and needs attention'. This statement demonstrated to me a capacity for psychological-mindedness, the possibility for him to articulate, gain distance from and understand holistically the multiplicity within his personality. It also showed his overall vision for himself in terms of wanting a more fulfilling experience of life. It felt important for me that I affirmed both his okayness and his vulnerability as valid experiences.

There were four main areas in which I wanted to gather more information from Jitu, to probe more deeply and to illicit further dynamic understanding for both of us.

Jitu's childhood

I wanted to get to know Jitu better as an adult and to hear how he described and framed his childhood. He stated that he 'wanted to understand the dynamics of a large extended family' and that the 'extended family is still very much a part of his life'.

Jitu's mother

In the initial interview, Jitu had spoken quite substantially about his father, but surprisingly little about his mother. I asked Jitu if he could tell me a little more about her, his relationship with her, what kind of person she is, and what role she specifically played within the family. He replied:

> My mother was the most significant, the most important
> person in my life. Certainly in my childhood and to a degree
> she is still an important person now. My early memories do
> give her a central role in my life . . . I'm not conscious of my
> mother directing me or controlling me, but I can see that
> she would have influenced me, she must have influenced me
> rather than told me to do things . . . I can't even remember
> how she cared for me, she must have done it so well. It
> never crossed my mind that she doesn't care for me. OK, I've
> had feelings about – momentary things – oh, she doesn't
> care for me in this situation, but I think overall she cared for
> me and she is the person I first went to if there is a
> problem. If she was available then I would go to her, but I
> can't remember going to her a lot. There was no need to . . . I

can remember her caring for me really, in all respects. Mind you, she was mainly physical care. Er . . . emotional care perhaps one did get. I can't remember not getting it. I can remember her washing me, doing things, making my clothes – or clothes for everybody in the family.

Jitu then went on to describe how competent his mother was with day-to-day life in the family, which was very large, Jitu being one of seven children. His mother obviously ran the family. Jitu stated that his mother was quite literate by Indian standards and that she made sure her children were too. He recognized that his mother was not the stereotype of the typical Asian woman, feeling that there was a very active life between his parents, 'not the public life' but rather a more sharing and open family life. Jitu's family seemed to be materially quite well off. His parents had worked extremely hard for their success and family's well-being. All the children were well educated.

Jitu's family

As Jitu had previously mentioned wanting to understand the dynamics of a large extended family, I went on to ask about his brothers and sisters, what role each played within the family and the cultural expectations he felt as a child. He spoke of one brother playing the role of the 'sickly one needing attention'. This brother apparently never ventured out of the family and still lives with their mother. Jitu mentioned here how his sisters were only important until they reached adolescence 'and then they are regarded as guests. Once they have reached the status of young women, rules start operating'. I assumed that here he meant cultural roles/rules, and noted this for future reference regarding Jitu's relationship with women. He also spoke of a younger brother being a 'non-entity – a quiet baby and an unnoticeable hard working adult'. The youngest brother was more like Jitu (who was the middle brother), an entertaining, charming and roguish figure.

Jitu's own family role apparently was one of 'being the mischievous one, or the naughty one, and the humorous one . . . Not that that was my entire role, but I definitely had that role at times'. I noted here his capacity to see himself as more than any particular role or style of being.

Coming to terms with mortality or death

It was in this area that I felt the death of Jitu's father to be significant, as a part of his expressed concern with the life transition to middle age and confronting his own mortality. It is often at this stage of life that unresolved grief issues from childhood emerge. How a child is encouraged to grieve, or not, is an important question when a death occurs in childhood. Jitu sensed that he was incomplete with his father's death when he was ten years old, and that he had 'work' to do in this area. He said, 'a central event in my life is the death of my father . . . I get glimpses and remember grieving at his loss, but I think essentially the process has been blocked out'.

I asked Jitu if he allowed himself to fully grieve his father's death. He answered: 'In retrospect I would say no . . . I have a premonition or a feeling that some of it is unresolved'. I asked him what messages he got from mother and family about how he should respond to his father's death. He replied that as far as both emotions and grief were concerned, 'these were mainly expressed by women, not the men. Men did their duty by being present at rituals but women were the master mind of the grieving process'. This, too, I noted as significant concerning Jitu's emotional life and his relationship with women.

An important aspect of working with loss is to express the unexpressed, complete unfinished communications and say what you have never said to the person who has died. I also asked Jitu if he had ever said goodbye, and appreciated his father for all that was precious in the relationship. Interestingly, he responded that he had done so more recently, as his work with people had brought him into embracing death and loss with his patients. I initiated a brief exploration of what gifts he felt his father gave him to help him be a whole person. Jitu noted that his father had given him the gift of 'letting him be himself', even though there were constraints. To him it felt good to be his father's son. He spoke of how his father taught him by example rather than by telling him things. He learned dedication from his father, dedication to work, to pursue success and to be a good person.

Jitu had three things that he would have liked to have said to his father. The first was that his father should not have allowed his brothers to tease him mercilessly, a feeling he had obviously carried for many years. The second was that he would have liked more direct advice on things in life. The third was that Jitu needed as a child to be more noticed as an individual, not just one of the sons. He felt that as a middle son, he was unimportant to a large family (though not less valued).

Jitu said that from the age of ten he had not really dealt with feelings, rather that he had had to act a certain role. I told him that this implied to me that there is a ten-year-old Jitu inside him that we would benefit from getting to know. I asked him if he was aware of this child inside and if he could describe him and his deeper needs to me. Laughingly Jitu said:

> I think he is very tall and lanky, very slim, much more
> becoming aware of himself now, for the first time, both as
> an individual and as a boy, or a boy about to enter
> adolescence. He was quite conscientious at school, with
> usually one close friend at a time.

He went on to describe how this ten-year-old Jitu needed to be looked after when his father died and to be acknowledged as an individual. The way little Jitu found to get his needs met was apparently through performing well at school, which gained him recognition in the family.

Cultural issues and influences

Jitu had several important concerns about cultural issues and how they affected his experience. He is an Indian, who grew up in Africa, living in an English culture. Also, he was married to an Irish woman.

I asked first about cultural expectations of him as a child. Here he identified that he had to do what was expected of him, to work hard and make his parents proud. And that once he had done that, he was expected to continue to do so: the family's good name was at stake should he not.

Regarding the cultural expectations of living in a foreign country, Jitu defined the adaptive part of himself, which is private and separate, although giving the impression of relating and connecting to people – a necessity in order to be approved of. He was very conscious of what he both likes and dislikes about the three cultures in which he has lived.

A bigger issue was the cultural differences between him and his wife. He said that in the initial years of their marriage, their differences had been exciting and challenging. In later years, it seemed to become a problem. Jitu implied that these cultural difficulties between them had made him long for his Indian roots, and that he had had to deny some important aspects of his own culture. He had felt unable to demonstrate his native culture's characteristics to his children. He implied that he had to hide certain cultural things from his wife and consequently from his children. He also stated how that was changing since his separation from his wife.

Traversing the middle stage of life and seeking meaning in life

Jitu had mentioned in his initial interview that he felt he was traversing the middle stage of life, which brought him in touch with his own mortality. He regarded this as a transitional phase in which he needed to learn to accept and cope with his limitations or imperfections and come to terms with mortality or death. He was also asking himself 'big' questions – about the meaning of life, about meaningless confusion, a lack of direction, a lack of connectedness. In psychosynthesis, these concerns are seen to be a part of the 'existential crisis' or 'crisis of meaning'. This crisis can and often does come with middle age when an individual has had success, has achieved many life-long goals and apparently has everything he needs to be happy. However, there is a lack: something essential is missing.

An important factor is how an individual responds to this crisis and what feelings it evokes. I asked Jitu how he felt about it all. His response was: 'frustration and disappointment in himself'. He felt that he should have realized earlier that he did not have to conform to society's attitudes and norms. He wisely saw that the only resolution of this for him was a 'spiritual one'. He said that he wanted to look beyond physical and mental appearances, for a reality that was deeper and fuller. He acknowledged that he often experiences an inner conflict between acceptance and grace in the second half of his life, the spiritual element, and the non-accepting more judgemental side of him, which resists imperfection and limitation. He noted how this non-acceptance gave him a deep sense of inadequacy and insecurity.

Finally, I remarked on Jitu's statements about searching for meaning and purpose. A 'deeper question of enlightenment . . . a questioning of what is real . . . many things must go beyond us to do with spiritual realization'. I invited Jitu to reflect on what was most meaningful to him in his life. He replied that his children were, and that his work had changed from being merely 'earning a living' to having a deeper dimension. As often is the case, the separation from his wife had propelled Jitu into this deeper consideration of what was meaningful to him. Nature, trees, being at ease with a good friend, music – these brought Jitu a sense of joy and well-being. I asked him what his motivation was for choosing to become a psychiatrist. Although on the surface his answer was, 'because it was difficult', underneath that he realized a desire to redeem his father's death, 'to be the son who saved him' and 'his own early experiences with illness'.

Assessment

I like Jitu. I appreciate his courage to question, his desire to understand himself more deeply, his unwillingness to accept what he does not value and his reaching for the spiritual dimension. He spoke of 'dharma', the ideal life pattern for each individual. He is searching for his dharma. The essence of the psychosynthesis perspective is that each of us has a purpose in life, and has challenges and obstacles to meet in order to fulfil that purpose. This purpose is analogous to a journey, in that we move forward along the path of life in a unique way and are always in the process of becoming. Each step forward contains the possibility of actualizing our potential. Along this journey we sometimes fall down, get lost or led astray, become stuck, move forward and make discoveries, or courageously travel beyond our limitations. For me Jitu is in the process of awakening to his own potential, to create a life for himself which in everyday ways is meaningful and fulfilling. Indeed, Jitu is a very healthy person.

With each of Jitu's presenting issues, he is reaching towards increased psychological health. Regarding his childhood, he knows that early conditioning continues to have an impact on his adult life, which is multidimensional and pervasive. He clearly has 'unfinished business' with his childhood through his realization that he is mentally identified and does not therefore always have access to his emotions. He also knows that his childhood was filled with being good, doing well for the family name, and dominated by the work ethic. In themselves these factors are not unhealthy, but when they are the dominant force, they can inhibit a child's overall development. Although he appears not to be fully conscious of it, the fact that he was one of so many children affected Jitu. He expressed this through his need to be seen more fully by his father as an individual, and to be approved of.

In psychosynthesis, the concept of the 'inner child' is one that is seen to affect profoundly the overall expression of ourselves in the world. If childhood experiences cause us to suppress aspects of ourselves, we lose authenticity for a compensating and defensive focus. 'Ten-year-old Jitu' needs Jitu's attention today. His father's death at this time, and later his brother's death, left something of the young Jitu behind. Cultural conditioning encouraged him to block his natural grieving process, evidenced by his comments about 'the women doing the grieving'. Jitu expressed feelings that he had blocked important aspects of his father's death, and that his death was 'like a shadow hanging over the family' today. Mid-life, and awareness of his own mortality, his brother's recent death, the death of extended family members and the current 'death' of his marriage, have all energized this issue for Jitu.

Jitu's relationship to women in general, and his mother more specifically, is an area for therapeutic work. The image I formed of her was of a loving and matriarchal figure who dominated the family life.

Jitu spoke highly of her skills as a caretaker (to me a rather mechan-
istic one, who showed ambivalence around her 'emotional skills'). I
noticed that any time Jitu said something which could be construed as critical towards his mother, he immediately countered it
with a positive statement about her. Being one of many children
bears influence here too. There was little time for mother to be more
than the efficient caretaker. The culture which Jitu belongs to also
affected his relationship with his mother: the expectations to do
well, to present the family in a good light, to be worthy and make
his parents proud.

What stands out to me here is that Jitu's own sense of identity
and individuality was not nurtured or particularly valued. There was
not a lot of freedom of choice – in the clothes he wore, the food
he ate and how he lived his life. He was proud to mention that
he brought African friends home despite his mother's disapproval.
Jitu mentioned twice the family story of being cared for (and special to) an African servant. He told how his mother negated this
story as a myth, as being unimportant, and that she was his mother.
I sense in the affect of this story, Jitu's need to be an individual and
to be special.

In terms of transference and counter-transference, I would pay
attention to a potential transference of wanting to be special, performing well for approval, fulfilling my expectations and generally
being a good client. I would also be watchful for the ambivalence
– hidden, but nonetheless dynamic. This might appear as coopera-
tion with subtle resistance or as an implicit undercurrent of rebellion.
I will need to be conscious of my own collusion with this through
affirming and encouraging the 'good boy' in our therapeutic work.
Will I respond as mother did? Will I subtly exert pressure to be a
certain way without evoking choice and identity? As a therapist, I
understand that my task is to encourage Jitu to find his own choices,
to evoke and affirm his individuality. I would very much like him
to lead the way in our work together, with me providing as few
interpretations and interventions as possible.

I see Jitu's search for meaning and purpose as the ground, the basic
context of our work together. Given the stage of his life, the inclusion
of this realm is essential and central to his well-being. The therapeutic
work will at best be merely adaptive, which is already a conscious
difficulty for Jitu, even without therapy. He demonstrates throughout
a deep yearning for the experience of unity: unity with himself, self-
respect, the experience of being a unique individual, a Self which
includes his personal life but goes beyond it. All this is central to his
yearning. I feel that Jitu's experience and expression of this deeper
identity will foster his evolution. Unity with others, the urge to love

and be loved, to deeply understand his relationships, and to heal through his work with others, are conscious aspirations.

Through his existential crisis, Jitu is being called to explore the realm of his creative potential and embrace his more spiritual drives. In psychosynthesis, spiritual drives or urges are seen as real, fundamental and indispensable needs as are the basic psychological ones. These deeper needs for self-realization must be met for optimum health. I will offer considerable focus on this area if Jitu continues to be responsive to his yearning. Jitu stated that the inclusion of (for want of a better word) a spiritual dimension was the only resolution to the reality of his approaching middle age and coming to terms with his own mortality. He expresses a desire to fully accept his own limitations and imperfections. His motivation to do this is eloquently expressed by his own words:

> I am toying with the idea of a spiritual dimension. I think the word is correct, because while I am aware of the spiritual dimension, intellectually, for it to be an experiential thing is a different thing altogether. I certainly have seen examples of a realized spiritual life, as opposed to an intellectualized spiritual life; and certainly I am not an example myself to myself. I wonder how one can jump into that area. It is like a dive, you know. It's like a risk you take. It is something that I want to have more meaning.

Therapeutic possibilities

There are several indications that psychosynthesis could be an appropriate psychotherapy for Jitu. As a 'mentally identified' person, the more active experiential techniques of psychosynthesis lend themselves to a deeper experience of his psyche. For Jitu the cognitive aspect needs to be complemented with experiential techniques, designed to evoke and explore deeper unconscious levels. Experiential work can uncover the historical roots of an issue as well as the creative possibility for change. It uses different modalities to work on an issue: the body and sensations, the emotions, the imagination and the intellect. The more modalities used, the more productive therapy will be. I believe that Jitu is ready to work at these more evocative levels.

Mental imagery is positively indicated. Imagery is the language of the unconscious and reveals in a symbolic way contents and conflicts which may be unavailable to the conscious self. It provides a means of communication with the vast reservoir of the unconscious. Through imagery, the myth-making capacity of the human mind has the opportunity for creating stories and events which pictorially represent the client's inner reality. Jitu could be awakened to new levels of himself through the use of mental imagery techniques.

When given the opportunity to question Jitu further, I asked that two experiential processes be carried out with him, both involving the use of imagery. Jitu felt positive about these experiences. One process put him in touch with both his deeper emotions and with a sense of what needed to be nurtured and developed in himself. Of the other, he said:

> it was a very relaxing and beautiful experience . . . it felt good and I would say a wonderful sort of experience . . . I must say this because normally I am a person who finds it difficult to sustain visualizations . . . but I feel different than when I came in . . . I must say I'm actually surprised by how relevant they are for me.

These two exploratory exercises, which Michael Jacobs conducted, gave me an indication of Jitu's openness both to his own unconscious and to the transpersonal dimension.

I am not presently aware of any serious contraindications for psychosynthesis therapy for Jitu. His basic psychological stability, his openness to and indeed desire for change, his longing for meaning, all indicate that at this existential moment it is appropriate to initiate a fundamental exploration of Jitu's psychospiritual journey. However, that is not to say that the process will be effortless. Academic training can be an obstacle to the more feminine, irrational levels of being. Jitu has spent much of his adult life in the role of an authority, the doctor who 'knows'. It might prove difficult for him to dis-identify from this partial identity and open himself to larger, more inclusive ones. A good dose of humility and capacity to embrace the unknown with no guarantees of security will be called for. The creativity of confusion will need to be respected. I suspect that Jitu has and is ready for these needed inner resources.

The course of therapy

Motivation

I will begin therapy with Jitu with a further exploration of what he actually wants from the work. The therapy can be as long or as short as Jitu wills it to be, depending on his presenting issues and stated goals. I experience Jitu possessing an underlying sense of his potential which beckons him towards health and wholeness: a primary need to take responsibility for his life and to experience it as valuable. These are potent motivating forces of which I want to evoke more conscious awareness. After this initial re-motivation, I will invite Jitu to make a choice to work together. I will frame this as a choice we both need to make. In psychosynthesis therapy, the fostering of the client's motivation is seen as a progressive series of steps leading to a clear intention for change.

My task is to evoke from Jitu a constructive awareness of what he really wants, to shift his motivation to conscious intention. This shift is made through evoking his will, and requires a shift from a negative orientation to a positive one. Initially, Jitu wants not to feel uncertain about the influence of his extended family on his life; not to feel incomplete with his father's death and his own mortality; not to feel he has to hide his culture from his wife and family; and, importantly, not to experience despair and life as meaningless. It involves clarifying what he wants to have happen and how he would like it to be with these 'not's'. Jitu comes to therapy with some degree of positive intention for change already mobilized. He has the psychological maturity to engage his intention. Intentionality implies a commitment from Jitu, an affirmation of his concern for his existence and a determination to do something about it. This will provide the strength for him to move despite resistances and the discomfort and pain which may be encountered along the way. No change is effortless and Jitu may need to live through a painful disintegration prior to a step forward.

Establishing a working hypothesis

As Jitu and I begin to establish a relationship, and hopefully have created a positive context upon which to build, I am now in a position to reflect more extensively on Jitu's unfoldment and create an overall working hypothesis. This working hypothesis applies to the macrocosm of Jitu's life and to the microcosm of any of his presenting issues. My perception of Jitu, unless addressed, will remain unconscious. Unless I address internally this perception, I risk losing sight of his individual uniqueness and imposing my own judgements of normative health. Hence it is both wise and practical for me to become aware of my working hypothesis for Jitu.

Emerging purpose

Psychosynthesis suggests that in a therapeutic relationship which fosters transformation and deeper well-being, the therapist will maintain a 'bifocal vision' of the client. Bifocal vision involves seeing Jitu from a dual perspective: first, as a Self, a Being with a purpose in life and an immense potential for love, intelligence and creativity; and second, as a personality, an individual made up of a unique blend of physical, emotional and mental characteristics.

Jitu has reported many issues and experiences which have prompted me to speculate: What is trying to emerge through these evolutionary steps forward that Jitu is seeking to make? What old behaviour patterns are dying in order for something new to be born? Emerging purpose is based on the idea that whatever is psychologically in the foreground for the client is not just conditioning or a pathological reality. Meaning is attributed to the fact that Jitu's particular issues are foreground difficulties: And what potential for growth is contained within them? What is there at this moment? Something new is trying to be born for Jitu. Emerging purpose is the progressive step forward contained within Jitu's difficulties. My task is to remain sensitive to this progressive thrust and listen to a level behind his presented content. Asking myself the above questions is perhaps more important than the answers I get.

The therapeutic relationship

With Jitu, I would see the therapeutic relationship as central and having an important influence on determining the outcome of therapy. This is partially because I am a woman and as such can provide the arena for Jitu to address his relationship with his mother, and come to terms with his childhood conditioning generally and specifically towards death and loss. We will look at what 'ten-year-old Jitu' needed but never received and explore his relationship with women. I suspect a lot of transference could operate underneath the surface of the work. Whether this transference will require being made explicit and directly confronted remains to be seen. Psychosynthesis, contrary to psychoanalysis, does not assume that transference is the centrepiece in psychotherapy, but that it warrants addressing only when it becomes an obstacle to the work. Transference can remain present, but will undergo changes as the client moves towards increasing maturity and independence, and as the human relationship grows stronger.

The quality of the therapeutic alliance between Jitu and myself will be at the very heart of the therapy. Without authentic relating, trust cannot be established between us; and without this essential ingredient, little true growth will be possible for Jitu.

Methods to adopt and adapt

Critical analysis

For the initial phase of therapy with Jitu, in order to establish a trusting therapeutic alliance, I will employ a psychosynthesis method of 'critical analysis'. Critical analysis is a method of active dialogue which can be used to assess both the blocks and potentials of the personality and to initiate an exploration of the unconscious in order to reach the roots of psychological complexes. As Jitu acknowledges himself to be a highly intellectual person, we will start with his mind, with observation and discrimination, to bring clearly into his consciousness the irrational elements of his issues and corresponding feelings. As I sense Jitu to be quite psychologically minded, I expect many insights could be gained through active dialogue.

Sub-personality work

I hypothesize that a primary area of both need and interest for Jitu is that of fostering identity and psychological freedom. Without a consistent sense of identity, there can be little self-acceptance or inner freedom. One's inner reality and outer behaviour are not congruent. Jitu's particular childhood conditioning, being a part of a large extended family and with cultural constraints, seemed to foster his adapting to the expected norms. I think a major limitation for Jitu is his identification with his persona or adapted self. This moment invites us to find a larger identity which can include his unique qualities and characteristics.

Sub-personalities are autonomous configurations within the personality as a whole. They are psychological identities, co-existing as a multitude of lives within one person; each with its own specific behaviour pattern and corresponding self-image, body posture, feelings and beliefs. In his interviews, Jitu had himself described as a 'ten-year-old boy' – the part of him whose development was arrested at his father's death. He speaks of feeling incomplete with his father's death at that time, of feeling confused and ambivalent. He also knew that this boy needed to be cared for and acknowledged as an individual.

Our work together needs to re-own and re-integrate the characteristics and qualities of ten-year-old Jitu. It is most likely that this sub-personality has much to contribute to Jitu's life. If he is treated with compassion and understanding, he can open up and give us the best of what he truly is. I am sure that working with ten-year-old Jitu will lead to working more with the death of his father, in order that he might fully grieve. This will open the flood-gates to the larger issue of death and immortality. I believe Jitu's issues around death and immortality are calling him towards a spiritual awakening of the meaning and purpose of his life.

Transpersonal work: self-identification

With Jitu, I would like to use several transpersonal methods of exploration, the first of which is self-identification. Identification with a sub-personality has been mentioned previously, but identification also occurs with psychological functions. In psychosynthesis terms, Jitu seems to be mentally identified, and tends to experience life at a more mental level. Psychosynthesis recognizes the mind as an instrument of experience, perception and action, but not as our essential core.

Our consciousness is rarely free or naked. It is always coloured with a feeling, a thought, a role or a sensation which we tend to experience as our Self. In the flow of the changing contents of consciousness, we lose our 'I', our true identity, our true Self. This Self is the factor which differentiates us from others, provides us with a sense of continuity and evokes our individuality. I want to work towards Jitu recognizing that who he is is much greater than his mind, than his role of psychiatrist, than ten-year-old Jitu, than his parents' son, or than his failed marriage.

Transpersonal work: the technique of inner dialogue

Inner dialogue is a guided imagery technique designed to address the client's existential difficulties. It is based on the hypothesis that each individual has within a source of self-love, understanding and wisdom that is in tune with our unfolding purpose and the next steps towards its fulfilment. Its aim is to enable the client to find his own answers, to be self-sufficient and to trust his inner wisdom. In my first interview with Jitu (through the editor), I asked that he have this guided imagery experience. The results were mentioned earlier, but suffice to say they were positive and uplifting for Jitu. He felt refreshed and invigorated by the experience. I feel inclined to pursue this work further with Jitu.

Transpersonal work: exploring life purpose

Given that Jitu is experiencing an existential crisis or crisis of meaning, I feel it important that we actively embrace this issue. First, we must embrace the existential 'now', the pain of meaninglessness and despair. Jitu feels a sense of transiting towards his own death and this brings feelings of frustration and non-acceptance. He is grasping for more, for life to contain some inherent and purposeful element.

Traditionally, psychological growth and the spiritual quest have been labelled as separate and essentially antagonistic directions. Freud and Western psychology rationalize spiritual pursuits as escapist or delusional and tend to view man's higher values and achievements as adaptations of lower instincts and drives. On the other hand, those following spiritual disciplines have often dismissed psychology as an unnecessary distraction. Psychosynthesis seeks to integrate these interdependent levels, and asserts them as complementary aspects necessary for the resolution of psychological issues and the awakening of the Self.

Given that Jitu found imagery work both possible and useful, after experience and understanding of the existential now, I will employ this technique to further deepen our exploration of meaning.

Problem areas

Authority issues

Jitu is a successful psychiatrist. This could present authority issues on two levels. First, will he be able to drop this identification and allow himself to be vulnerable and the one seeking help? There is a strong conditioning for doctors in all cultures, to always know and be fully in charge; yet being a client requires that we have the courage not to know, to acknowledge our insecurities, our uncertainties, to embrace the unknown. Jitu and I will need to be watchful of this authority identity controlling the therapeutic work. It will also challenge my counter-transference, to trust myself and not surrender to 'doctor knows best'.

This issue could also arise through Jitu expecting *me* to be the authority. I am the psychotherapist and I should have all the right answers to his dilemmas, confusions and queries about life and himself. Will Jitu expect the answers to lie with me as the authority, rather than within his own psyche and inner wisdom? Will he trust himself to have the necessary inner resources? Or will there be resistance to this? I believe this will be further evoked through Jitu's transference towards me, which could take the form of unconsciously wanting me to be this wondrously capable mother who was always in control and made sure life worked well. Will Jitu relinquish his power to me and will I subsequently be able to empower Jitu? If authority issues arise, their resolution will be an essential part of the therapy.

Potential to let go

Jitu has outgrown his identity. His self-image is limiting him. His adaptive personality is no longer serving him. His life feels empty and meaningless. These realities point to Jitu being invited to let go of outmoded and obsolete ways of living and being. He is aware of these factors, but does he have the will to let them go, in a sense to let them die? Probably not, until he comes to terms with loss and death and mortality. We can understand any resistance Jitu might have. Letting go is like a little death, the death of an identity. Identities which we have had for a long time were initially developed for a purpose, usually as a way to cope with our life situation. They have served us well and provided some sense of meaning. To let them go may feel like losing an old friend. Fear of a deep void or inner emptiness may accompany the potential loss of an identity. Although the letting go ultimately leads to inner freedom and a deepened sense of identity, Jitu may temporarily feel more vulnerable without the old one.

Cultural influence

Jitu and I between us have five cultures operating – Indian, African, Italian, British and American. This presents us both with a challenge to stay conscious of how these cultures are manifesting, both through our relationship and through the therapy. We both might have personal biases and limited perceptions operating. Jitu's attitude towards women could become a significant factor in our therapeutic relationship. I may not fit his images and ascribed roles for women, nor will I necessarily conform to his hopes and expectations. My own culture is perhaps one that encourages a freer expression of feelings and emotions. Will I become impatient with Jitu's inhibitions? However, in today's multi-cultural world, we both have substantial experience to call upon.

Criteria for successful outcome

Psychotherapy is an open-ended journey. There is no moment which indicates that the work is finally complete or after which Jitu is guaranteed happiness and well-being. Self-realization is a process rather than an end result. There will always be unmanifest potential, a next step for Jitu in actualizing himself. Therapy will hopefully build his resources, increasingly enabling him to work creatively with his subjective and objective process. Jitu is clear on the areas of concern and work in which he would like to engage. Rather than think of the resolution of these issues as our goal, I deem it important that Jitu develops the skills and inner resources to address them.

Jitu expressed the desire to experience himself as something much more permanent, not to continue to feel fragmented. He spoke of wanting to reach a plateau, an image which he loved. This statement is a clear indication for transpersonal work – for finding the stable sense of Self and identity mentioned throughout this chapter. Jitu's subjective experience of reaching a plateau will show us that he has reached a place of relative inner freedom and stability. However, it is vital that Jitu recognizes that this plateau will not be a permanent experience, but an indication of being on the right track for him, a signpost along the way.

From my perspective as therapist, the successful outcome may be described as an expanded sense of identity, an increased acceptance of all life experience, an integration between inner and outer worlds, a revelation of meaning and the discovery of purpose. These notions seem congruent with Jitu's comments of what he would envision for himself in therapy:

> to be at peace with myself and certainly one of the elements is coming to terms with the past . . . much more accepting of myself, less pushing myself into how I want to be, more accepting as to what is there . . . but not excluding the imperative to develop, to grow.

Regarding a successful outcome for therapy, Jitu said:

> I don't agree with the term satisfactory conclusion . . . I think it would be like getting on a train and getting off, to get on some other train if you like . . . Therapy would just be a means of accelerating you along the sort of direction you want to go anyway . . . I think therapy would be like buying a ticket and seeing where it takes you, not necessarily a destination in mind.

In psychosynthesis, the answer to a satisfactory conclusion is determined by the client. In dialogue with me, Jitu will regularly assess our work and determine its continuation and eventual termination. Jitu's answer leaves the door open for us to continue for as long as he experiences the work valuable, and as long as he is motivated to continue. It is common for a psychosynthesis therapist to initiate periodic reviews of the work. These serve several functions. They afford the opportunity for client and therapist to examine their therapeutic relationship and to assess the client's progress. They also provide the occasion to consider the advisability of concluding. Although I will offer feedback and evaluation when appropriate, Jitu himself will lead the way and define the boundaries for finishing.

Further reading

Assagioli, R. (1965). *Psychosynthesis: A Manual of Principles and Techniques.* New York: Viking Press.
Assagioli, R. (1973). *The Act of Will.* New York: Penguin.

Ferrucci, P. (1982). *What We May Be.* Wellingborough: Thorsons.
Ferrucci, P. (1990). *Inevitable Grace.* Wellingborough: Thorsons.
Hardy, J. (1987). *Psychology with a Soul.* London: Routledge and Kegan Paul.
Whitmore, D. (1986). *A Guide to the Joy of Learning: Psychosynthesis in Education.* Wellingborough: Thorsons.
Whitmore, D. (1991). *Psychosynthesis Counselling in Action.* London: Sage.

10

MICHAEL JACOBS AND JITENDRA

REVIEW AND RESPONSE

Selecting the types of therapy that would be most relevant for Jitu was particularly interesting. My recognition of the cross-cultural issues made it essential that there was at least one therapist of the same ethnic background as Jitu, if for no other reason than to make a comparison with the interpretations made by white therapists of Jitu's issues. Josna Pankhania turned out to have an almost identical experience to Jitu's, of African as well as Indian and British culture, making her an especially suitable therapist to include in this book. Four of the remaining therapies were identified as having special significance in cross-cultural matters. First, Jungian analytical psychology, because Jung himself drew upon Eastern as well as Western religion and philosophy, and was himself interested in the religious dimension (questions of the meaning of life seemed to be on Jitu's mind). Second, psychosynthesis, itself having some connections with Jungian thought, is clearly one of the transpersonal psychotherapies, again keen to embrace the feelings and thoughts of the Eastern mind as much as the Western. Third, a therapist who was also a Buddhist seemed to me to provide another dimension to the religious aspect of this case. In a sense, the clinical psychologist label is irrelevant: it is that other faith system, which itself grew out of Hindu religion, which is particularly interesting when linked with therapy. Fourth, Lacanian psychoanalysis was relevant because it is the product of another European culture, and presents a Gallic way of thinking that sometimes seems so different from British pragmatism. I did not justify the inclusion of personal construct therapy on any particular grounds to do with this case; but it was essential to have this contribution to complete the series, representing as it does a major psychological theory in its own right, and a particular and distinct section of the UK Council for Psychotherapy.

This particular volume took even longer to complete than the others in the series. Four of the therapists made the most of the opportunity of seeking further information from the client, leading to pages of questions for me to put to Jitu, covering every aspect of his early life and adolescence as well as the present. He and I met for many hours, taping the conversations, which in subsequent transcripts proved a very rich source of reflection for Jitu himself. The extended time necessary for this put back the project and cut across the carefully prepared timetables of some of the authors, who had thought they would be able to write their contributions earlier than was the case. These delays meant that their contributions came in at very different points of the year that followed, providing Jitu with the opportunity of thinking in depth upon each one. He read them through many times. He and I met for two interviews to reflect upon the formulations of the six therapists, and upon the experience as a whole. Overall, he felt that each of them was saying similar things from their own perspective. His earliest, perhaps over-generous, response was that none of them had missed anything.

I set out his more specific responses here in the order in which we talked about them, although this is not the order in which they appear in this book. When making comparisons and contrasting the different contributions, Jitu and I ranged back and forth over them all, before he told me which one represented the therapy to which he was most attracted, and the one which, were he to decide to go into therapy, he thought he might choose.

Christopher Perry

Jitu's immediate response to this chapter was 'accurate' and 'very helpful – I couldn't quibble with him on anything': if Burgoyne is right in his chapter in identifying the obsessional in Jitu, then 'quibbles' might of course be expected. Perry's was one of the contributions that appealed to Jitu the most. He was not sure, however, whether 'the Jungian analyst', as he tended to call him, would really be familiar with his culture. Jitu likes Jung, and realizes that a lot of his ideas are from the East; but the language Perry uses would be a second language to Jitu, it would not be his native language for the same concept. He made the same point about Burgoyne's sharply worked use of language. The therapist will therefore need a different constellation of words to start empathizing with him. Jitu felt he would not have the sophistication to tell the therapist where he needed to modify his view. I myself felt that he would not be at all averse to doing this, since Jitu seemed not to be afraid of being outspoken when he was with me; and he did say that as a psychiatrist he would be observing his therapist as much as his therapist was analysing him. I also wondered whether Jitu would be more questioning of a male therapist than of a female therapist. My question took Jitu by surprise, but he thought I might be right. The women who worked on his material he saw differently: 'wasn't Diana a goddess, or something', he asked at this point. Jitu had said, in response to one of Perry's original questions, that he would prefer to work with a woman rather than a man, and preferably an Indian woman.

I observed that Perry thought that he might have to refer Jitu to an Indian woman therapist, but someone who was in touch with her masculine side (the animus, in Jungian terms). Jitu felt that such a referral would be letting him down. Perry hinted at the possibility of a twice weekly group, although to Jitu this felt more like managing a problem and not relating to him. He also considered the additional suggested possibility of family therapy alongside individual therapy, and this did not seem like a rejection. Indeed, Jitu felt Perry was in this suggestion tackling the 'here-and-now' in a way that none of the others did, and that this was sensitive of him. He had realized that Jitu was going through a special process in the family splitting up. Jitu was very moved that Perry was the only one who thought of his children. In fact Pankhania had too, but when I reminded him, it was clear that this had failed to register with him.

However, Perry also suggested addressing the inner world of this client in addition to the external factors, and that in seeking an Indian woman Jitu was seeking, outside himself, somebody whom he really needed to find inside himself. The gender and the culture of the therapist might therefore not be relevant: what would matter would be that the therapist could assist Jitu to find the internal figure whom he felt he needed. Jitu said that it was only through this project that the Indian woman in his fantasy had been internalized. He had been fascinated by Indian women whom he met at different functions, and he had rich imaginings and projections about Indian women. But this had disappeared, like the sun coming out melts the mist, and he had replaced his own inner fantasies with a more realistic perception of such women.

Like Whitmore, Perry suggested he might use other forms of expression, such as modelling and painting. This was a new dimension to Jungian therapy that I had not myself realized (except more directly in relation to psychoanalytic art therapy). Whereas in Whitmore's chapter these methods felt an integral part of her work, in Perry's chapter Jitu thought this was a technique for connecting; but he thought he would go along with it, and engage with it, once put in that situation. He would need his therapist to connect it with whatever else he was doing. I wondered whether what worried Jitu was that such techniques might be revealing, and that he might not like what was revealed.

Perry distinguished the possibility of 'shame' in Jitu. This initially upset him when he read it, although he thought there was truth in it, and that it was very relevant. It fits, of course, in a Freudian typology, with the obsessional characteristics which Burgoyne identifies in Jitu, although Perry stresses introversion as the major aspect of Jitu's personal typology. Jitu's intellectualizing may be an expression of his obsessionality from Burgoyne's perspective, but it is a way of relieving depression in Perry's analysis of Jitu's pathology. Like Burgoyne, Perry refers to Oedipal issues, especially identifying the possibility that marrying outside his culture was a defence against his incestuous wishes – feelings which might also have been split off when he was young in his attachment to the African woman.

Perry observed how much Jitu had used the de-personalizing form 'one', and that he appeared to be disconnected from his feelings. He had also suggested that since he himself was more a 'feeling' person and Jitu more a 'thinking' person – opposing types in the Jungian typology – Jitu might not like him probing his feelings. Jitu agreed that he is a thinking person, although he also has feelings, and he thought that he might find Perry uncomfortable because he would not collude with him. At the same time, Jitu felt that such refusal to collude with him would be a necessity in therapy. Jitu also felt that he would be valued by this therapist 'in a deep sense', citing the end of the chapter, where Perry ended on the note that there is nothing that Jitu does not know, and much that he as the therapist does not know. There is an interesting contrast here with the other psychoanalytic therapy in this book, Lacanian psychoanalysis, where Burgoyne refers to the analyst's need to work constantly to overcome the resistance, because unconscious connections do not readily seek the light of day. Jungian thought often has a more favourable view of the capacity of the unconscious to find expression, whereas Freudian thought emphasizes the repression of unconscious material.

The therapist's lack of knowledge was not so apparent in Perry's identification of several feelings in Jitu: sadness, rage, anger, loneliness, loving feelings, joy, excitement, dependence and competitiveness. These were indeed feelings that Jitu recognized in himself, and he liked the way that 'good and bad were put together', although he was surprised that Perry had identified competitiveness, because it is 'not a feeling in my book'. Nevertheless, Jitu admitted that there might be such feelings in him which he did not recognize. He thought it was true that love and rage got embedded together in him. He talked more about love, and his difficulty telling friends that he loves them. He prefers to call it caring, but his friends express their love, and do not like it when he cannot use that word. Jitu worries that if he uses the term 'love' he does not really mean it, and if he does not really mean it or does not live up to it, that brings shame: 'Shame, love, rage and anger are all mixed up inside'. It is only his children with whom he feels he can really use the word 'love'. To love is to risk being hurt, since the person he loves may die.

Perry thought that he and Jitu might work well together since they share a belief in a higher wisdom. When I checked out whether Jitu felt the same, he became rather intellectual in his response, questioning the idea of 'higher', although he moved into a happy memory of his view of God as a child, a smiling blue man (like Krishna, but not Krishna) in the sky with a big belly.

Josna Pankhania

Jitu 'liked' this therapist. He felt that Pankhania would be very good in specific areas, where European therapists might not understand him. She had used the phrase, 'Jitu's story is my story', although she was conscious of the danger that she might over-identify with him. Jitu felt that there would be some familiarity between them from the start. He also noted that hers is a mixed marriage too, and he 'would find that very interesting', although he thought that an Indian woman adapts to a man in such a situation better than an Indian man does to a woman, partly because women are better at holding contradictions together in themselves. He was certain that although he may have intellectually absorbed Western values, and acquired certain intellectual constructs, he had not necessarily internalized these: 'your emotional life works on a different plane altogether'. He might have expected more of his wife than was possible: their relationship could not be like his own parents' way of relating.

Pankhania is of course an Indian woman therapist, such as Jitu had told Christopher Perry he thought he would prefer to see, although, as he explained above, this need had shifted in its intensity in the course of the project. Jitu felt Pankhania to be a 'very astute woman', and he liked her awareness of the dynamics, of immigration, and of living in another culture. He believed that she would be able to do a lot of productive work with him in this very important area of his life, which most of the others could not do by definition – at least this was his fantasy. There were other ways in which she identified and shared with Jitu. The question of grief Jitu felt was universal, but the other griefs in life might need to be examined: in his marriage, for example, his grief 'was the continual loss of your self demonstrated daily in little moments – the grief of not being yourself, of not being allowed to speak your language, or validate your religion or family – now I can be myself again'. It is this which he thought Pankhania might pick up. Jitu thought that generally the therapists had failed to address the marriage, which had been a major and lengthy part of his life. The inability of him and his ex-wife to integrate two cultures continued to be 'a sore spot'.

Pankhania suggested that she might like to help Jitu conduct a ritual for his father, at which she might or might not herself be present. If he were to do this, he thought he might be able to do this with her, because she would know the rituals. As he spoke, Jitu reflected that he may indeed need to be able to do this, because he had not been to the funeral. Since the project had started, he had had a few conversations with his father in his mind, had sworn at him, and acknowledged his feelings for him. In some senses he was not so present. He had done his own rituals, not in a ritualized way, but he had said:

Look, it's time that I said goodbye to you – you've bothered me long enough. But of course you know that I loved you and cared for you. I am a father like you and I must look after my children, and sometimes I will come back and tell you what I think.

Because he is a father to his own children, Jitu felt he did not miss his father so much now.

This felt a deeply caring chapter. Pankhania described her reaction to Jitu as 'one of wonder, great respect and sadness', although she spotted like the other therapists just how cerebral Jitu is, and there could be difficulties with him blocking emotions. She clearly sensed what pain there might be underneath the surface, since she found it 'difficult to write about how painful this grief may be for Jitu'. She was also concerned for the children, in a way that the others apparently were not – even if Fransella had asked a question about their number and ages, and Perry had considered the possibility of family therapy for this particular life crisis. Jitu felt that Pankhania did not concentrate enough upon the cultural aspect of his marital relationship. She did not bring the macrocosm of the societal dimension into the microcosm of the marriage; indeed, perhaps one of the curiosities of her contribution is that, starting as she does from a political perspective, she fails to address political issues, but concentrates almost solely upon the individual client. It seemed to the two of us, as we talked about this, that Pankhania had brought in the social and the cultural more than the political. As far as Jitu was concerned, her awareness of oppression was important.

For a person-centred therapist, which is part of Pankhania's background, she asked a remarkable number of questions about Jitu's childhood. In fact, her wish to go into such detail was as great as Burgoyne's, although the latter used detailed knowledge to look at unconscious connections and the way Jitu constructed his history, whereas by contrast Pankhania dwelt more upon the overt material in this history, and the way the history might now influence him. Jitu very much liked the way she summarized his life history, which he felt she had done with considerable skill.

When at the end of her chapter Pankhania wished Jitu 'goodbye', Jitu had felt he wanted to meet her – at that point he felt very sad in his reading of her contribution. It was a sensitive account, in which she showed obvious concern for Jitu, and how her questions might affect him. He thought he would like to have engaged with her in therapy, in order to test certain things out with her, even though she was not his 'number one choice'. He knew that they would speak the same language, and that they could talk.

Fay Fransella

Jitu liked this contribution very much. There was something about 'Get down to it, and let's work at it' in her approach which he had not felt with any of the others. He works very easily with intellectual concepts. He thought he would get some very unusual work done with her, and that it would be real. He admired and deeply respected her. He thought she had put together some of his experience 'beautifully'.

Fransella, like Rothwell, asked hardly any questions, although she asked him to engage in two short exercises in which he looked at various aspects of his self-image and his age. What is particularly noticeable about her contribution is that she does not make a hard and fast distinction, as virtually everyone else does, between thinking and feeling. It does not matter to her that Jitu tends to be intellectual, although she notes that emotions do not figure in his self-characterization. 'Who you are is who you *think* you are, as well as who you *feel* you are', said Jitu as he began to talk about her chapter.

Jitu thought this form of therapy did not allow sufficiently for the unconscious side, which is an important concept for him, although I noted that at one point Fransella almost equates pre-verbal issues with a notion of 'unconscious', or in personal construct terms 'a low level of cognitive awareness'. There are, however, no 'dynamics' attached to this concept, and she does not append the definite article '*the* unconscious' as psychoanalytic and psychodynamic therapists do. She acknowledges the value of dreams, and Jitu and I felt it was a pity that she had not asked about *his* dreams, because he could have given her, as he gave those who asked, his dream of the black cat.

Nevertheless, what appealed to Jitu was that she would view him from a scientific view, as 'an animal', constructing a proper hypothesis. At this point in our review, Jitu started to talk about Popperian views of science, becoming very academic. He began to argue with some of her positions. I sensed some danger in giving Jitu too much permission to go with his head, since the intellectual side of him began to dominate. It is not clear from Fransella's account, in which she integrates thinking and feeling aspects, how she might deal with what some other therapists would call this type of intellectual defence.

Jitu did not think he would break down in front of her, as he might in front of the others, but he felt that she would help him to look at how he sees the world. He had a sense of her having a commitment and faith in her system, and that he would have a choice with her whether he wanted to fit in with it or not. Jitu recognized that he could easily play a therapist's game, although he hoped that having taken part in this project he would be less liable to do that. He also felt that it was easy for people to collude with him, but that Fransella was right to say that he had to have control over events. Her contribution had led to him feeling that he does not allow himself to be a full human being: he does not have immediate and full emotional reactions to human events, like deaths or celebrations, although he remembered a time when he had been much more spontaneous. He agreed that he identified with his professional roles, and he needed to let some of that go, although at another point in our review he said that he had ceased dressing like a psychiatrist – he did not now wear a suit and tie in his daily work.

Jitu felt he could bring anything to this therapist, and that she would try and identify the problem. She would analyse it, as she does in the diagrams she drew, which I observed bore some similarity to his own self-description, which was itself almost set out in a diagrammatic form. Jitu was impressed by the way she draws his material together in the diagrams of the tightrope and the overarching construct. 'Impressed', I said, 'But was it helpful?' He thought so. The diagrams illustrate that he is, as Fransella suggests, 'the expert on himself'. The design may be her own, but she gives no answers of her own, instead drawing upon the raw material Jitu has presented to her.

She also lists four aspects which might trap him: pre-verbal issues; lack of identity and lack of understanding of others; fragmented sub-systems in his constructs (are these like the sub-personalities mentioned by both Perry and Whitmore?); and being a victim of his own biography. It was quite painful for him to consider a possible lack of identity: 'it winded me, like a punch'. She notes that Jitu does not ask what his wife's agenda might be; in fact, he said, he had asked her this many times, but never got an answer. Fransella thought that it might be difficult for him to see things from others' perspectives, which he thought was so.

What I found interesting about our review of this chapter was that Jitu did not pick up on the material which Fransella makes very obvious about his childhood; for example, like Burgoyne, she notes the possible significance of him being a member of a large family. She also refers to the way in which the young child self in Jitu was unable to develop, and there are several paragraphs in which his childhood experience is stressed. None of this did he respond to in his reading of her approach: he dwelt on the scientific and the hypothetical. Personal construct therapy clearly integrates thinking and feeling, and does not wish to set them in conflict with each other. But with a client or patient in whom this defence predominates, I was left with the impression that a personal construct therapist would have to work hard to ensure that the construct did not crowd out the personal. This is no doubt a simplistic way of putting it, and personal construct therapy clearly does *not* make this division. But Jitu was capable of exploiting the emphasis on constructing hypotheses. What was 'beautiful' may have been the unintended neatness of the diagrams rather than the tensions they described.

Fransella and Rothwell both suggest a shorter period of therapy. In Fransella's case it is eight one-hour sessions. This appealed to Jitu, because 'at this moment' he wanted a minimum engagement: 'I don't like the idea of ongoing therapy'. But he hoped the eight sessions would be a minimum: 'three months, a year' seemed to be his preference. He experienced himself as changing all the time.

Her short final paragraph mentions the cultural differences between herself as the therapist and Jitu as the client. He felt this was tacked on, a sort of 'by the way remark', and was to be contrasted with Perry and Whitmore, who attach much greater weight to this potential difficulty in the therapeutic relationship.

Neil Rothwell

Jitu liked this therapist very much as a person from the way he could imagine him to be when he first read through his contribution, but he felt that Rothwell focused too much on the religious and the spiritual. If Jitu had 'any quibble with any of the therapists it was with this one, since it was too wishy-washy for my liking. He was too much in the air. It sounds nice, but it just doesn't connect'. This last word is an interesting choice, given the title of this book. Jitu could not in the end engage with Rothwell. This was not because Jitu is a Hindu, although he admitted that there are some ideas in Buddhism which are alien to Hinduism, and he was drawn more to Zen than to 'Buddhist nature'. The phrase 'Buddha Nature' did not do anything for him. Whether there are genuine differences in Zen I do not know, but Jitu felt it strongly, and became more antipathetic to Buddhism as the interview went on. Buddhism, for example, is very austere in terms of the absence of gods and deities. Jitu did not think that a Buddhist could understand a Hindu like him as much as a Hindu therapist such as Josna Pankhania could, although as we talked further Jitu became quite vehemently opposed to any type of therapy which calls itself either Buddhist, Hindu or Christian. Indeed, I began to think it was his encountering their brush with 'Christian counselling' in some of his patients that had so turned his mind against this chapter, even though Rothwell did not in any way advocate an overtly religious approach. Jitu himself thought he might have some kind of negative transference to Rothwell's approach.

Jitu recognized that Buddhism is the most psychological of all religions, and that it is about the realization of being fully human. But Jitu felt that he would have to fit in with Rothwell's scheme of things, whereas he felt the others were listening to him. I suspect this was a mis-reading of Rothwell's chapter, coming from some other anxiety in Jitu. He rationalized this by saying that for him Buddhism does not fit with the discipline of psychotherapy.

My own reading of the chapter was more favourable. I picked up that Rothwell would try to understand Jitu from within a Buddhist framework, and that as a therapist he would try to adopt a meditative attitude; but I had no sense that he would be seeking to impose Buddhism on the client. Jitu thought he might have a block in trying to relate to this therapy, and wondered if in reality therapy with Rothwell might be different, in that the therapist would bring other things to the session not discussed in his chapter. Jitu imagined that he might be a 'truly inspired person', but thought that in this chapter trying to write about religion did not work.

It was not this aspect that had concerned me. I was myself puzzled by the person-centred start to Rothwell's contribution, and then its shift into a solution-focused strategy. Jitu and I took very different views on this: it was the problem-solving aspect that was more interesting to him. I noted too the difference between most therapists indicating that they want to help anger to be expressed, whereas Rothwell talks more of accepting anger – something which Jitu fully understood and to some extent agreed with. There is some validity in this, he thought. He explained that there is too much in the counselling world about people having a right to their feelings, so they are encouraged to think they are being assertive when they are in fact being aggressive. He liked it that anger should not be either over-valued or under-valued. Jitu saw Rothwell as a counter-balance to counsellors and therapists (he instanced Gestalt therapy) who give too much attention to feelings, and who can give rise to 'pretty destructive behaviour' in some of their clients. Jitu had again seen this in some of the patients in his psychiatric practice.

Rothwell suggests six sessions (like Fay Fransella proposes eight sessions). Jitu thought this might be all right, although it would depend on how the sessions went: 'As an initial contract that would be OK'. Rothwell also suggested that the frequency of the sessions should be determined by Jitu, an idea I found related to some of Winnicott's work, such as with the little girl called the Piggle, who was seen at intervals of several weeks, virtually 'on demand'. I was also fascinated in Rothwell's use of the break, in which towards the end of the session he leaves the room for five minutes, leaving the client on his own, and highlights four of five points that he made in his notes during the session, returning to give this feedback to the client. Jitu, obviously thinking with his psychiatrist's hat on, was not at all sure that he wanted 'a progress report'. Neither did he think much about the idea that he might come when he wants to, which I thought might appeal to him, given his response to Fransella, that he is not at all sure about therapy which extends beyond a year. If Rothwell had been a priest, Jitu could go and see him in this way, but he saw psychotherapists as having a professionalism which rendered this type of arrangement uncomfortable, even given Rothwell's permission to see him in that way. It is important to go regularly if he is to be helped maximally, because he is not the sort of person who would go to see someone when he felt vulnerable and raw – 'that's the least time I would want to go'.

Despite the solution-focused aspect that appears in the second part of this chapter, Rothwell stresses how much the client takes the initiative. Not only is the frequency of the sessions determined by the client, but it is also the client who chooses what he or she wants to share. It is perhaps significant that Rothwell asks so few questions of Jitu, because it is not his style to impose his thinking or his questions on the client. This is another point where I imagined a Buddhist attitude fitting more obviously with a person-centred approach than with solution-focused therapy. Rothwell is happy for the therapy to unfold in its own way: he suggests no particular activities such as painting (Perry), self-characterization (Fransella), performing a ritual (Pankhania) or imaginative exercises (Whitmore). Rothwell's questions do not seek the detailed history of Pankhania's or Burgoyne's. For Jitu, who wants some structure, and perhaps even a diagnosis in which he can feel safe, perhaps this therapy, which is generally much less defined, could only be caricatured by him as 'wishy-washy'. Jitu is uncomfortable with something so fluid, however much, as in this case, the openness is a quite deliberate therapeutic approach, and not the result of any confused thinking.

Diana Whitmore

It was initially 'the Jungian and Diana' (as Jitu put it) 'that appealed the most', the latter offering the most comprehensive picture. Of all the therapists involved with him, it was for her for whom he felt 'the deepest respect' (a word which Jitu uses with great feeling but also with some frequency):

I get the feeling of a really solid woman . . . she knows what she sees, and can put words to it. She captures things, and I like her view of the person. She has this idea of the Divine, of the Self, of the inner world.

Although Whitmore would not be as familiar with his culture as Pankhania, he felt she would overcome that handicap, in a way that the other European therapists might not. He liked her name – he referred to her throughout as 'Diana', more frequently using her first name than he did with the other therapists. He admitted that she appealed more to his fantasy of what a therapist should be, although I would want to add (and Burgoyne's chapter supports this) that I think she appealed to his fantasy of what a woman should be.

The comprehensiveness of the cultural mix that would be present in her therapy with Jitu again appealed – this was 'complete'. She includes herself in this, which again appealed to him. The adjectives 'comprehensive' and 'complete' often appeared in his responses to this chapter. Whitmore's formulation seemed to hold him together: he felt she could take anything on board. She takes up the religious quest, but not to the exclusion of other things (Jitu was concerned that in Rothwell the religious quest was everything). He also thought she would be very demanding, and that she would not let him hide behind his spiritual quest. She writes that the spiritual dimension would be 'the basic context of our work together', but presumably this would indeed be the context, and not necessarily in the foreground. She would go into feelings. She had spotted that his self-image is limiting, and he knows that too: 'it is a terrible burden to have this image of yourself'. As in Perry, and to some extent using slightly different terms ('sub-systems of constructs') in Fransella, Whitmore refers to sub-personalities and to the loss of the inner child, whom Whitmore describes as 'a very shadowy figure'. He was not sure how sub-personalities related to 'personality', and I was myself not clear what the distinction is between the 'Self' and 'personality'. Sub-personalities seemed to me similar to the internalized figures (aspects of parents, aspects of self) described in psychoanalytic object relations theory.

Whitmore wondered whether Jitu's mother had been rather mechanical in her mothering. Jitu was reluctant to discuss this. In the first place, he had recognized (as Whitmore suggested) that he often followed a negative remark with a positive one, so he had to say 'I do not know'; but he was also concerned with what he saw in the counselling and therapy world as a knocking of parents. His mother is old. In his concern for her, he showed that closeness which Burgoyne in his chapter had surmised was often consciously denied by Jitu, especially in describing his childhood.

Whitmore refers to the possibility that she will have to address Jitu's relationship with women. She expects a lot of transference in this area, although she is not sure that it will need to be made explicit. Of course, the positive transference can often be accepted without any need to comment, so that it forms the basis of the working relationship. However, what was clear to me in Jitu's response to Whitmore was that this transference was already in place, and that it was a positive one which might need to be examined, because it veered towards idealization; indeed, the very idealization which Burgoyne clearly identifies in Jitu's view of women. At one point, Jitu referred to the image of Whitmore in his mind as being 'larger than life'. Whitmore anticipates that the transference might be one in which Jitu wants to be special. My impression was that he had already made her very special: he isolated a number of features in her work that also appear in Perry, Fransella, Pankhania as well as in Rothwell (to whose therapeutic approach Jitu had not much taken, but in whom, for example, the spiritual quest and openness to him were seen to be as clearly present as in Whitmore). Perhaps it was, as he said in using the words 'complete' and 'comprehensive', that all this came together in Whitmore's chapter; but I would hazard a guess that some of his enthusiasm (which in its Greek roots means being taken over by the divine) was indeed because he had made her divine. 'I am maybe building her up', he said. She struck me as much more rooted in reality!

I put to Jitu the possibility of such an idealized transference towards Whitmore, and he became for a short while rather defensive about the descriptions he had used of her. Diana, I reminded him too, was the goddess of the hunt, which amused him greatly! (She was also the goddess of the moon and of virginity.) He thought that in time he would become more aware of his negative feelings towards her, and he would read her again in the light of my observation, 'to get a balanced view of things'. 'There is a transference', he admitted, 'and we would have to work with it'. It is useful to note that Perry also surmised that 'Jitu will form a positive transference to me both developmentally and archetypally'.

Whitmore herself sees that she has to be careful in her counter-transference not to collude with Jitu, a caution which Burgoyne expressed in an aside to me in a letter, where he commented that Jitu's analyst would have to be 'on guard' not to be seduced by just how 'very likeable' Jitu is. Burgoyne does not in fact refer to the counter-transference at all in his chapter. Perry's two references are more general and do not specifically refer to the impact Jitu might make on him, although Perry does write that he and Jitu could find each other difficult since their 'superior functions are opposite', Perry's being feeling, whereas Jitu's is thinking. This could of course also be described as a counter-transference difficulty, if rather the opposite to the counter-transference collusion which Whitmore and Burgoyne each consider likely to occur unless they are very careful.

I asked Jitu how he felt about working with the different modalities in therapy which Whitmore suggested she might use – for example, working with the body, with sensations and with the imagination. He told me how much had been achieved when he had gone through her exercises at the second stage of the project. He recalled that he had been resistant to drawing when I had first asked him to take part in one of the exercises which Whitmore had proposed I conduct with him. He is still resistant to such an approach, and he has a little difficulty in seeing how this activity is connected to his unconscious.

In concluding our review of Whitmore's contribution, Jitu and I went over what it was about her that so attracted him: she acknowledges the cultural dimension in its entirety; she includes herself in the process; there is a comprehensiveness about her approach; she recognizes the importance of the question of meaning; she would engage Jitu in a number of exercises and be challenging to him; and she would not let him get away with things (Diana the huntress!). 'On the face of it I would engage with *her* as first line, and see how it works in reality'.

Bernard Burgoyne

Burgoyne's chapter was the last one which Jitu received. It therefore came at a stage when he had in his own mind put Whitmore as his first choice. What was fascinating to Jitu and myself was the way in which, coming when it did, Burgoyne's analysis made some sense of what already felt like a 'larger than life' response to Diana Whitmore.

Jitu started, however, by describing Burgoyne's contribution as 'clever and very relevant'. Burgoyne puts the Oedipus conflict much to the fore and in Jitu's words, 'he played with it much of the time'. At times on the first reading both he and I had found it hard going, because of the complexity of the thinking; and sometimes we had thought that Burgoyne might be making too much of the use of particular words. It seemed at first that Burgoyne was over-simplifying the issues by attributing everything to the Oedipus complex. But on re-reading the scenario it became more convincing, because it held together and ultimately it made much sense to Jitu. It was the sheer detail which meant you could not avoid taking notice.

Jitu's 'quibble' with this was to do with different languages and cultures. He agreed fundamentally that there is a connection between what is 'instinctual' and with the external language and culture. But he thought that Burgoyne assumed that English was his first language, and he queried whether Burgoyne was basing what he wrote on a Western concept of relationships. Against this I reminded Jitu that the same principles apply to any language (for example, words have either consistent meanings, or can be used with different meanings in any language) and that what Burgoyne was doing was comparing and contrasting is Jitu's own use of language. It does not matter whether English is a first or a second language: Jitu uses words in different places with same (or different) meanings. In that sense, all our words are constructions, used in similar (or different ways) by any one person: it is the therapist's task to listen for how one person uses key words and phrases, even if (or even because) they use them differently from another person.

There is perhaps some similarity with personal constructs here, although Fransella and Burgoyne would need to say whether there is something in common about the way they understand language. I suspect that Lacanian psychoanalysis, as in its Freudian origins, sees words as pointers, indeed as 'signifiers', to deeper connections in the unconscious, to which I imagine personal construct therapists do not attach such importance. I noted too in Burgoyne's account how it is not actual history that appears to matter, but Jitu's *construction* of his history, even if Burgoyne acknowledges the way Jitu's history has also constructed him. Both Jitu and I remembered just how much he had valued being able to tell this history to me, as I worked my way through Burgoyne's (and Pankhania's) extensive and often overlapping questions about his childhood and his adolescence. What had been notably different in the two sets of questions was that

Burgoyne had also asked in great detail about Jitu's father's and mother's own parents, and even about the generation beyond that.

Burgoyne therefore analyses Jitu's own use of words, and the constructions he puts upon his own history and his parents' history, in order to make his interpretations about him. Jitu wondered whether the values in an Indian family might differ from the Western interpretation being put upon him and his history: How did the Oedipus complex fit with larger families, where grandmothers, for example, perform the motherly role? Jitu thought that the Oedipus complex might be more applicable to the nuclear family. Nevertheless, if the situation is not identical, the idealization of the mother, the other women and the absent father all made great sense to him. We noted that Burgoyne's stress throughout is on the absent father (not on the *death* of the father as Jitu originally framed the issue, since the death was only one aspect of the father's absence); and even more Burgoyne stresses the love (desire) for the mother. Jitu felt that Burgoyne had made all this more conscious for him: 'He knew me more than I did' (quite a contrast to his equally enthusiastic reaction to Perry's final statement that Jitu knew himself better than Perry did!). 'I think it is very accurate, and I think it touches on a very important part of my life, on my relationship with my mother and my father, and how the other women come into it'.

The more he read it the more Jitu thought Burgoyne was right, and he did not quibble with this 'really deep work': 'This was the real issue – it must be because it explains a lot in the present. It is a valid hypothesis, and you have got to work at it'. Jitu felt that 'that particular phantasy's back had to be broken because it definitely is handicapping me in my relationships – having this need to idealize. Although I said there was this need for the feminine guidance, that was another form of this idealization'. What Burgoyne also did was to throw light on how much Diana Whitmore has also become an idealized figure for Jitu. I wondered whether Burgoyne appealed because his approach seemed very intellectual, and might be like solving a puzzle, something which Jitu enjoys. Jitu replied that there was, for example, a difference between Burgoyne and Fransella: 'He doesn't say it, but I feel he would bring the complex alive each time, and the feelings would be so powerful. He would just wait for them to crash out rather than pointing out my denials of them'. Jitu recognized that working through the meaning of words did not just involve thinking. When Burgoyne drives the significance of a word home, Jitu is led to feel, 'Oh God, it is true . . . Basically this chapter has broken my resistance to the complex'.

There is a remarkable confidence about Burgoyne's chapter. We noted that he had made an initial assessment of Jitu before he asked any further questions, and that his detailed questions (of which there were many) seemed designed to test the hypothesis out, rather than to gain more material in order to make a hypothesis. Jitu observed that Burgoyne was 'far from being person-centred' – he thought at times he had been fitted into a scheme, although he could not quibble with the fit that had been made. My own sense was that Burgoyne *had* been person-centred in that he had analysed Jitu's *own* words in that very first session in utmost detail. What is also remarkable is how accurate (judging by Jitu's response) he appears to have been in this initial assessment. It is of course legitimate to ask whether the analyst's confidence persuades the analysand of its correctness. When he writes, 'Jitendra is clearly obsessional. I will take him on', it sounded to Jitu like a military order, and on first reading this almost put him off reading further. He would have liked a little more sign of doubt (one of the features which Burgoyne identifies as strong in Jitu) and of tentativeness in the way he makes interpretations.

Jitu went on to spell out the accuracy of Burgoyne's analysis in more detail. It is true that he has 'hang-ups about love relationships' and about the ideal object. The list of the signs of his obsessionality was accurate: doubts, looking for certainties, isolations and idealizations, ambivalence in close relationships, generalizing, wanting to be in control. All this was true. These factors are becoming worse as time goes on. Jitu found it difficult to give up the idea of a search for perfection. He felt that the definition of the obsessional was clearer in the chapter than the definition of 'hysteric', which seems to be a technical term, and more than what Jitu thought it meant: that Burgoyne wanted him to become more emotional. He did not agree that he suffered 'loss of desire' in the 'slightest aspect of the other person . . . it can be the positioning of a hair, or the angle of a fingernail'. He knew it in others, but not in himself.

One phrase which Jitu used was that Burgoyne had 'taken him by surprise'. This led us to reflect on the way Burgoyne writes of ending sessions at a significant point, rather than by the hour of the clock. This way of working, which is unique to Lacanian analysis, seems to finish sessions at the point where the analysand is 'taken by surprise', leaving the person to go on working on it, on their own, rather than risking diluting or obscuring the breakthrough of unconscious material by continuing to a fixed end of the session. In this way, Jitu felt, you do not relieve the person of the tension of this fresh insight. It must be a very effective way of emphasizing how important that moment of revelation has been. I wondered what Jitu made of the suggestion that they might need to work together for seven or eight years, meeting anything between one and six times a week, and perhaps if he was travelling to London from Birmingham, two or three sessions a day. Jitu laughed: 'Forget it'. He said that it was not practicable, and in the long term not affordable (something I doubted given his salary, although the question of time was perhaps a difficult one for him). Nevertheless, I put it to him hypothetically: 'If you had the money and the time, would you be attracted to this form of therapy?' 'Yes, I would', he replied. But he remained hesitant whether he would continue over such a long time.

Jitu could see how they could work together, but he was left puzzled by what the solution would be. I reminded Jitu that Burgoyne had written in the last paragraph of the need at the end to break the 'power of the phantasy' that gets in the way of 'all of Jitendra's love relationships'. This appealed to Jitu as an aim, and he also liked the very last phrase that 'at the end of this analysis, Jitendra can conclude something about his desire'. This touched a chord in him, particularly the term 'desire', since it linked for him to a word for 'desire' in his own culture called 'kāma': 'In the beginning there was desire, when the world was created'. Burgoyne had picked up on the deep desire to relate to mother, and he liked that.

What was both curious and fascinating was that at this point of our final interview, Jitu had used the Sanskrit word 'kāma', which is pronounced like the English 'calm' (i.e. the first 'a' is long and the second 'a' is silent). He used a term identical in sound therefore to that used in the enigmatic sentence in Burgoyne's chapter: 'Jitendra's calm contains a claim on his father's wife' (p. 30). While it may at first be thought that Jitu was here responding by associating what he had read in Burgoyne's chapter and the Sanskrit term 'desire' because it links with the Lacanian interest in 'desire', I need to point out to the reader that when I sent Jitu Burgoyne's chapter I thought there was a typing error and I had therefore altered the phrase to read 'Jitendra's *claim* contains a claim on his father's wife'. Only later did I get confirmation from Burgoyne that 'calm' was indeed the word he had intended, by which time Jitu had already introduced his own term 'kāma', intricately but unawares linking his own thought therefore to Burgoyne's. This was a coincidence perhaps, but a strange one.

In the end Burgoyne had 'an intellectual rigour which appeals to me, and it is so new, so different, so surprising that it would be difficult to say "no" to him. . . . He obviously sees more, and sees accurately'. Jitu wanted to revise his earlier premature assessment: whereas Whitmore had initially been 'first line', and he would still want to have the chance of working in that way, it now seemed that Burgoyne's analysis had achieved the same rank as hers in his list of preferences. To produce an order is of course invidious, and Jitendra did not intend to do that, because he also knew what most appealed to him in each of these therapists. Nevertheless, there is some rivalry implicit in this whole project, and in concluding our review with this Lacanian perspective, such preferences as Jitu expressed should not be avoided.

I felt, as I drew the final session with Jitendra to a close, that in fact each of the therapists in this book had in specific ways thrown more light upon each other's ways of understanding the client than perhaps in any of the books to date. They each shared at least one major idea or interpretation in common with at least one other therapy; but the connecting lines were not neat, and the connections between them led to a real network of ideas that as a whole helped to make the entire project, as Jitendra stated as he left the room for the last time, 'a real privilege'.

Conclusion

From reading my initial interview with Jitu, Diana Whitmore's first concern was Jitu's motivation. He had opened the very first hour with the words:

> It's difficult to say anything at this point of time, partly
> because one's feeling relatively OK, but there have been
> times when things have been more depressing, where one
> can talk about that fairly clearly and with meaning.

She picked up well both his sense of being 'relatively OK', and the times when he was 'vulnerable and needs attention'. She felt that his motivation was good; and of course in our review of the six therapists, Jitu made it clear that he would be very prepared to work with her, as indeed he would with most of the therapists. My own perception of him, however, throughout our time together, is that Jitu shows much greater ambivalence than either Whitmore or indeed any of the other therapists recognized. He was completely engaged in the project, and was indeed fascinated by it and by what he learned about himself. But I was aware that when he was 'relatively OK' he did not feel like entering therapy, and that when he felt vulnerable he might not find it easy to seek help. He had said this in response to Rothwell's offer of sessions on demand. I suspect he tends to go inside himself, as ten-year-old Jitu did, and would require a good deal of coaxing out.

At the conclusion of our review, I asked Jitu whether he would now be more inclined to engage in therapy. The project 'had persuaded him, though not by intellectual argument', he said, that this could be valuable: 'my resistance has been neutralized'. He recognized that he does not give himself the time 'to do this kind of work', but he had valued the many pages of transcripts of our tapes and the six therapists' contributions: 'I will be reading them time and again over the next two years'. Therapy would be a massive undertaking, and he 'might have to be forced into it by a catastrophe'. He felt that Whitmore might have recognized that possibility, which was another reason why he was drawn to her, since he felt he could trust her in such circumstances.

Jitu said that he would be more likely to know whom he would want to work had he met the therapists face-to-face. This is of course the same difficulty experienced by all the therapists in this series, which is not surprising when nearly every psychotherapeutic approach is based upon the meeting and interaction of two or more people. The only general criticism Jitu made was that he felt that they had not dealt with the problem of evil, 'anything within you that does not allow you to develop'. My own opinion is that in relation to his definition of evil, in one way or another most of the therapists had addressed the blocks inside him, whether they referred to defences, being trapped, or to other particular terms. Rothwell mentioned the word, but he did not see 'the world as divided fundamentally between good and evil'. Fransella discussed evil more fully, and it was indeed only in relation to her questions and her request for his self-characterization that Jitu's struggle with good and evil in the cosmos and within himself emerged. Neither the word nor the issues appear in the original interview. The other therapists did not see this part because it was specific to Fransella alone, and therefore they cannot be expected to know its importance for Jitu. As it was, I felt that Fransella addressed the issue as an inner psychological state – she refers explicitly to this in a whole paragraph, including the phrase 'perhaps all too often he finds himself behaving in an "evil" way, which has very serious implications and no doubt leads to feelings of loss of control and of chaos, decay and death'. I suspect she would not have felt discussion of objective and external 'good and evil' was relevant, except as a pointer to innermost psychological constructs and ideation.

Jitu wanted to emphasize how much respect he had for all six therapists, and how much he had benefited from these people telling him things about himself in this context:

> It is a deeply enriching experience for me, potentially more
> so, because each time I read them it is a different focus. This
> is something I come back to over and over again. I am never
> bored with this. Sometimes they hurt me with one or two

things, and at other times I am very intellectual studying myself like a third person [Perry had drawn out the observer role which Jitu takes up], and it doesn't touch me. But I am grateful.

He had valued the contact with me: 'Our meetings are deeply connecting, and it seems to go on working in me for a long time afterwards'. He had found the process exhausting, because at times he had not had a lot of reserves in himself. He felt that he was more aware of avoiding issues in himself and that he would have to make his mind up about seeking therapy – not because of the pain, but because of the need that had been identified. He is good at avoiding catastrophe, but at other levels there is a lot of agony, meaningless and restlessness – nothing to do with other people, but deep within himself.

Jitu felt deeply privileged to have had so many people engaged with him. He had said much that he would never say to anyone else, but he felt that he had been honest. He thought he had come forward for this project to tackle the shame in him, and because he did not believe that it was good to remain a private individual. One of the people who had most influenced Jitu was Gandhi, who himself had tried not to become a private individual. 'There is a lot of excitement in things being a secret, but once you expose them I think you become more human. I am learning to live with that shame'.

Like the other four people who have been central to *In Search of a Therapist* – Charlie, Peta, Morag and Ruth – Jitendra has made himself very public. Like them he is disguised by the alteration of all his major identifying features; but most of his life – and the lives of the other four 'clients' – has been exposed to the scrutiny of twenty-nine different therapists as well as the gaze of thousands of readers. This is a strange sensation for people – clients and therapists alike – who normally are so private. It is of course right that therapists should allow public scrutiny of what they do, although that is very difficult given the privacy which clients rightly expect.

Inevitably, all these contributions raise further questions; and readers who wish to, can clearly follow up their interests in the books suggested at the end of each chapter. There is no way in which I and my co-editor can conclude this series neatly, because of the many issues about the various forms of therapy – twenty-seven in total – but we can endorse the words of all five clients, of the deep gratitude that they and we have felt at the willingness of all these therapists to expose their personal approach to critical attention. The willingness of the clients themselves to share much of their experience, past and present, and for most of their secrets to be uncovered, has enabled some steps to be taken to allow those of us outside the therapy session (including other therapists) to have a clearer sense of what might go on within it. In the end, those who deserve our greatest appreciation – for helping us all to look at the relationship of theory to practice, at the way in which we work, and at the claims we make – are these five people who have been in search of a therapist.

MORAG – MYSELF OR MOTHER HEN?

Moira Walker (ed.)

I don't like cleaning and hoovering and washing up. I do them because I have to, and I feel that James wants me to be in the house, to be there because his children are there, and the family's there . . . he likes me there being the mother-hen!

This is how Morag begins to tell her story to her potential therapist. Six therapists are given the opportunity of assessing Morag: What do they wish to know about her? How might they work with her? And what outcome can they predict for her as a result of therapy?

In this highly original book – which starts with Morag's own story – the reader has a chance to see six different therapists at work, drawing on the same material from the one real client. The similarities and differences between therapies are highlighted. And at the end the reader is able to enter Morag's experience of the process, and decide with her, which one she might choose in her search for a therapist.

This fascinating volume will appeal to a wide range of students and practitioners involved in counselling and psychotherapy, particularly those interested in comparing different therapeutic approaches.

Contents
The editors: in search of the client – Morag: myself or mother hen? – The reader's response – Roxanne Agnew: focused expressive psychotherapy – Windy Dryden: rational emotive behaviour therapy – Paul Holmes: psychodrama – Arthur Jonathan: existential psychotherapy – Anthea Millar: Adlerian therapy – Peter Savage: hypnotherapy – Moira Walker and Morag: review and response.

Contributors
Roxanne Agnew, Windy Dryden, Paul Holmes, Arthur Jonathan, Anthea Millar, Peter Savage.

176pp   0 335 19224 6 (paperback)

PETA – A FEMINIST'S PROBLEM WITH MEN

Moira Walker (ed.)

'I've got a problem with men . . . I don't know whether it's a problem with other things as well . . . I am afraid of what men represent . . . I feel they have more power.'

This is how Peta begins to tell her story to her potential therapist. Six therapists are given the opportunity of assessing Peta: What do they wish to know about her? How do they understand her? How might they work with her? And what outcome can they predict for her as a result of therapy?

In this fascinating book – which starts with Peta's own story – the reader has the chance to see six different therapists at work, drawing on the same initial material from the one real client. The similarities and differences between therapies and therapists are highlighted. And at the end the reader is able to enter Peta's experience of the process, and decide with her, which one she might choose in her search for a therapist.

This highly original volume will appeal to a wide range of students and practitioners involved in counselling and psychotherapy, particularly those interested in comparing different therapeutic approaches.

Contents
The editors: in search of the client – Peta: a feminist's problem with men – The reader's response – Jennifer Mackewn: Gestalt psychotherapy – Judy Moore: person-centred pychotherapy – John Ormrod: cognitive behaviour therapy – John Rowan: humanistic and integrative psychotherapy – Maye Taylor: feminist psychotherapy – Christine Wood: art therapy – Moira Walker and Peta: review and response.

Contributors
Jennifer Mackewn, Judy Moore, John Ormrod, John Rowan, Maye Taylor, Christine Wood.

168pp   0 335 19223 8 (paperback)

CHARLIE – AN UNWANTED CHILD?

Michael Jacobs (ed.)

'All the while I very much got the impression when I was young that my mother didn't love me and doesn't love me. I think of myself as unlovable . . .'

These are Charlie's opening words to her potential therapist. Six therapists are given the opportunity of assessing Charlie: what do they wish to know about her? How do they understand her? How might they work with her? And what outcome can they predict for her as a result of therapy?

In this fascinating book – which starts with Charlie's own story – the reader has the chance to see six different therapists at work, drawing on the same initial material from the one real client. The similarities and differences between therapies and therapists are highlighted. And at the end the reader is able to enter Charlie's experience of the process, and decide with her, which one she might choose in her search for a therapist.

This highly original volume will appeal to a wide range of students and practitioners involved in counselling and psychotherapy, particularly those interested in comparing different therapeutic approaches.

Contents

The editors: in search of the client – Charlie: an unwanted child? – The reader's response – Cassie Cooper: Kleinian psychotherapy – Phil Lapworth: transactional analysis – Frank Margison: psychoanalytic psychotherapy – Alix Pirani: humanistic-transpersonal psychotherapy – Anthony Ryle: cognitive-analytic therapy – Claire Wintram: feminist group therapy – Michael Jacobs and Charlie: review and response.

Contributors

Cassie Cooper, Phil Lapworth, Frank Margison, Alix Pirani, Anthony Ryle, Claire Wintram.

176pp   0 335 19199 1 (paperback)